W.H.D. ROUSE was one of the great twentieth-century experts on Ancient Greece, and headmaster of the Perse School, Cambridge, England, for twenty-six years. Under his leadership the school became widely known for the successful teaching of Greek and Latin as spoken languages. He derived his knowledge of the Greeks not only from his wide studies of classical literature, but also by traveling extensively in Greece. He died in 1950.

GODS, HEROES AND MEN OF ANCIENT GREECE

W.H.D. ROUSE

NEW AMERICAN LIBRARY

New American Library
Published by New American Library, a division of
Penguin Group (USA) Inc., 375 Hudson Street,
New York, New York 10014, USA
Penguin Group (Canada), 90 Eglinton Avenue East, Suite 700, Toronto,
Ontario M4P 2Y3, Canada (a division of Pearson Penguin Canada Inc.)
Penguin Books Ltd., 80 Strand, London WC2R 0RL, England
Penguin Ireland, 25 St. Stephen's Green, Dublin 2,
Ireland (a division of Penguin Books Ltd.)
Penguin Group (Australia), 250 Camberwell Road, Camberwell, Victoria 3124,
Australia (a division of Pearson Australia Group Pty. Ltd.)
Penguin Books India Pvt. Ltd., 11 Community Centre, Panchsheel Park,
New Delhi - 110 017, India
Penguin Group (NZ), 67 Apollo Drive, Rosedale, North Shore 0632,
New Zealand (a division of Pearson New Zealand Ltd.)
Penguin Books (South Africa) (Pty.) Ltd., 24 Sturdee Avenue,
Rosebank, Johannesburg 2196, South Africa

Penguin Books Ltd, Registered Offices:
80 Strand, London WC2R 0RL, England

Published by New American Library, a division of Penguin Group (USA) Inc.
Originally published in a Mentor edition.

First New American Library Printing, March 2001
20

 REGISTERED TRADEMARK—MARCA REGISTRADA

LIBRARY OF CONGRESS CATALOGING-IN-PUBLICATION DATA:
Rouse, W.H.D. (William Henry Denham), 1863–1950.
    Gods, heroes and men of ancient Greece : mythology's great tales of valor and
romance / W.H.D. Rouse.
       p. cm.
Originally published: New York: Mentor, 1957.
Includes index.
ISBN 978-0-451-52790-5
    1. Mythology, Greek. I. Title.
BL782.R68 2001
398.2'0938'01—dc21   00-048197

Printed in the United States of America

PUBLISHER'S NOTE
The publisher does not have any control over and does not assume responsibility for
author or third-party Web sites or their content.

The scanning, uploading and distribution of this book via the Internet or via any
other means without the permission of the publisher is illegal and punishable by law.
Please purchase only authorized electronic editions, and do not participate in or
encourage electronic piracy of copyrighted materials. Your support of the author's
rights is appreciated.

DEDICATED
TO THE INTELLIGENT BOYS
OF THE PERSE SCHOOL, CAMBRIDGE,
WHO LISTENED TO THESE STORIES
AND WHEN THEY HEARD A GOOD THING
KNEW THAT IT WAS GOOD

CONTENTS

NOTE

This book was first published in England in 1934 by John Murray Ltd. The changes of 23 years have made some minor alterations necessary, and the Pronouncing Index has been added. Otherwise the book remains as it was written, a lively and entertaining account of the ancient Greek legends, by a scholar eminently qualified to write it.

My cousin Dr. Rouse, who died in 1950, was Headmaster of the Perse School, Cambridge, for 26 years, and under his leadership the School became widely known for the successful teaching of Greek and Latin by the "Direct Method," as spoken languages. He was a man of great industry, who took for himself the Choice of Herculês (page 56):

Nothing that is really good can be got without labour and hardship, for so the gods have ordained.

He derived his knowledge of the Greeks not only from his wide studies of classical literature, but also from many holidays spent travelling in Greece, in the early days alone and later with the Hellenic Travellers Club. Speaking modern as well as ancient Greek he made many Greek friends; he sailed with the islanders in their sailing craft, and listened to their tales and folklore.

This delightful book is written in an easy style, and as the author proceeds he takes his readers into his confidence (page 166):

You see, they [Achillês and King Agamemnon] had both lost their temper. I do not make any excuse for either of them; I am just telling the story.

I venture to commend it to readers young and old.

—*Philip G. Rouse*

PREFACE

These stories were told to Perse School boys, and they have gained by the boys' criticism, conscious or unconscious.

The stories are told as parts of a connected whole, as the Greeks felt them to be, although no doubt each knew his local legends best. The genealogical chart at the end may be useful for reference. That comes chiefly from Hesiod; but the authors whom I have used range from Homer to Nonnus. If I have sometimes drawn on my imagination for the dialogues, so did Homer and Nonnus; and so did the Greek nannies when they told the stories to their nurslings.

—W.H.D. Rouse

INTRODUCTION

When you hear these stories of the Greek gods, you must be careful not to confuse them with your own God, for although the same name is used, it means different things. The Greeks thought the world was managed by a multitude of beings, like another human world in general but consisting of beings who had different powers from men. The chief of these were very powerful, and the little ones had greater power than men. They loved and hated and quarrelled with each other, like men, they even fought battles, like men, and one dynasty of kings supplanted another; but they could not kill each other, for they were immortal—they could only kill the monsters and giants who were also commonly to be found. And all these were themselves subject to something higher than themselves, which they called Necessity. It is this highest power of all that we call God, and the Greeks were feeling their way towards it, but they thought less about it than they did about the lower powers. These stories concern these lower powers and how they were mixed up with mankind.

Many of the Greek stories are beautiful, but not all; and they seem to say that the gods rose out of savages just as men did, and learnt by degrees what was good and noble. All these stories fit into a picture, where each has its place. The Greeks knew them well, and they are always taken for granted at the back of their minds; so that without them we cannot understand the Greeks at all. The ordinary people believed them, as European peasants believe the stories of the Saints. They thought of the gods as friendly creatures, rather like themselves, who enjoyed a bit of fun as much as they did; but they also feared them as terrible and strong and ready to punish wrong-doing. By degrees the wisest of the Greeks looked for a meaning in these stories, and did not believe them exactly; they thought of them as poetry, or fairy tales. But their ideas of right and wrong were much the same as ours, and they revered all that was good in their gods as much as we revere our own God.

PART 1

I. *The Beginning of Things*

In the beginning there was Chaos, a great hollow Void, in which the seeds or beginnings of all things were mixed up together in a shapeless mass, all moving about in all directions. By degrees these beginnings slowly sorted themselves out; the heavier parts gathered together, and became Earth; the lighter parts flew up, and became the sky, with air between; and under the earth was a dark place called Tartaros. In the heavens, the sun, moon, and stars appeared one by one; on earth, the land separated from the sea; rain fell, and the rivers ran down from the hills; trees grew up, and the world became something like what we know, and it had the shape of a great round ball, or a disk, like a large plate.

From Chaos, the great Void, came forth many and strange children; but first and most wonderful of all was Eros, or Love, who came no one knows how, and was quite different from all the others; he outlived them all, and still lives, the most mighty of all divine powers. From Chaos came forth also Erebos, and black Night; and their child was the Day.

From Chaos, lastly, came into being Father Uranos, or Heaven; and Pontos, the Sea; and Mother Earth. Heaven and Earth were parents of a great brood of children. These were called, in general, the Titans. The brood began with monsters, but they improved as they went on. Among the monsters were three, with fifty heads apiece, and a hundred hands; their names were Cottos, Gyas, and Briareos. Three others were named the Cyclôpês; Cyclops means Goggle-eye, and each Cyclops had one huge eye in the middle of his forehead, with one huge and bushy eyebrow above it.

11

There were others, some of whom we shall meet later; and then came a superior brood of children. I will not tell you the names of all these now, but one was Oceanos, the ocean-stream, which runs like a great river all round the earth; and one was Hyperion, who took charge of the light by night and day. He was the father of Eos, the Dawn, and Helios, the Sun, and Selênê, the Moon. And the youngest of the children of Heaven and Earth was named Cronos: the youngest, but the most terrible of them all.

Now Uranos hated his children, and feared them; and as each was born, he hid them in secret places of the earth, and kept them prisoners in darkness. But Mother Earth was angry to see her children so badly treated: so she persuaded them to rebel, and they did so, and cast down Uranos from the sky. They cast him down into Tartaros, the dark region below the earth. In the fight he was wounded by Cronos; drops of his blood fell on the sea, and from these drops sprang up Aphroditê, who became the goddess of beauty and love. Her name means daughter of the foam, because she came up out of the foam of the sea. Other drops of his blood fell on the earth; and from these sprang up the Giants and the Furies. We shall hear of these later: for the Giants made war on the gods long afterwards; and the Furies used to range about the world, when men were created, chasing and punishing those men who shed blood.

Cronos was leader of this rebellion, and he became King of Heaven in his father's place. When he became king he cast down his brothers and sisters into Tartaros, except one, Rheia, whom he married. But he was not so careful about their children. Some of them were useful, like Dawn, and Sun, and Moon, so he left them alone. Another of the Titans had five sons. Atlas was one of those sons, and he was made to stand by the gate of Tartaros, and to hold up the sky on his shoulders. Two others of this family were very famous afterwards. Their names were Prometheus and Epimetheus, that is to say, Forethought and Afterthought. Prometheus was the cleverest of all the Titans; and he went to live on the earth. There he used to wander about making models out of mud to amuse himself.

Now at that time things were not quite sorted out from Chaos, and there were bits of life still in the mud or clay of the earth. So when Prometheus made this clay into all sorts of odd shapes, the shapes came alive as he made them, and became worms, and snakes, and crocodiles, and all kinds of strange creatures, which you can see in museums. As he grew more skilful, he made also birds, and animals, and at last he thought he could make something in the shape of the immortals. His first attempt went on four legs, like the other animals, and had a tail like them—it was a monkey in fact. He tried all sorts of monkeys, big and small, until he found out how to make his model stand upright. Then he cut off the tail, and lengthened the thumbs of the hands, and twisted them inwards. That may seem a very little thing, but it makes all the difference between a monkey's hands and a man's; just try and see how many things you cannot do, if you tie your thumb fast to your first finger. And if you look at the skeleton of a man in the museum, you will see that you have a tiny tail in the right place, or at least the bones of it, all that is left after Prometheus cut it off.

Thousands of years afterwards, the Greeks used to show in one of their temples lumps of clay, which they said were left over after Prometheus had made the first man. This clay was the colour of mud, and smelt a little like human flesh.

Prometheus was very much pleased with his new pet. He used to watch men hunting for food, and living in caves and holes, like ants or badgers. He determined to educate men as well as he could, and he was always their friend. Cronos did not take notice of what he was doing; and now we must turn to Cronos, and see what he was doing himself.

II. *The Gods*

Cronos had married one of the Titans, named Rheia; and he was determined that his children should not rebel against him, as he had rebelled against his father, so as soon as one was born, he swallowed it whole. Five he swallowed up in this way; but then Rheia grew tired of this, as she wanted babies to play with, so when the sixth was born, she determined to save him. She took a big stone of the same size as a baby, and wrapped it in swaddling clothes, and presented it to Cronos as the last baby. Cronos promptly swallowed the stone, and was quite contented. This was really a thing easy to manage, because no doubt the gods used to do with their babies just as the Greek mothers used to do; they wrapped them round and round with a long narrow cloth, until they looked like a chrysalis, or a long plum, with the baby's head sticking out of the end. Then Rheia took the real baby, whose name was Zeus, and hid him on the island of Crete, in a cave which you can still see at this day. He was put in the charge of two nymphs, who fed him on goat's milk, and the cave was watched by armed guards; whenever the baby cried, the guards made such a din by clashing their spears on their shields, that Cronos heard nothing of its cries.

Rheia bided her time; and when Zeus grew up, she told him how Cronos had swallowed his brothers and sisters, and how she had saved Zeus himself; and they made a plot against Cronos, as Cronos had done against his father. Together they managed to give Cronos a strong dose of medicine. This made Cronos very sick, and he disgorged all the children, one after another. First came the stone which Rheia had made him swallow; and Cronos was very much surprised to see that. You may see the stone, if you wish, for it was placed in the sacred place of Delphi, and it is still there, in the Museum. Then came the five others in order. I must tell you their names now, because they all come into the story; they were Hestia, Demeter, Hera, Hadês, and Poseidon. Strange to say, they had all grown up quite well inside their father, and now they were as big as Zeus, and ready to join in the plot. Then they all made war upon Cronos, and the war went on for ten years, but neither party could win.

Cronos got friends to help him, as far as he could, and one of them was the wise Prometheus. As the war went on, Prometheus said, "Sir, I advise you to bring up your brothers from Tartaros." But Cronos was afraid of his brothers: he said, "No, thank you, no brothers for me." When Prometheus found that Cronos was too stupid to take good advice, he went over to the side of Zeus. To Zeus he gave the same advice; and although Zeus was not very wise, he was wise enough to take this advice. So he set free the three Cyclôpês, named Thunderer, Lightener, and Shiner; and they were so grateful, that they gave Zeus a gift each—the thunder, and the lightning, and the thunderbolt. They also gave Hadês a cap, which made him invisible when he put it on; and they gave Poseidon a trident, or three-pronged spear. Next Zeus set free the three monsters with fifty heads and a hundred hands. You see what an advantage that gave to Zeus. Each of them was like a quick-firing gun, and could throw a hundred stones for Cronos's one.

Now Zeus made a feast for his friends. He gave them nectar, the drink of the gods, and ambrosia, the food of the gods, which was the food of immortality; and he said, "Now let us fight, and make an end of this long war."

Then there was a terrible battle. The three monsters caught up a rock in each of their three hundred hands, and cast them in volleys at Cronos. Zeus thundered and lightened and launched his thunderbolts. The earth shook, the sea boiled, the forests caught fire and burnt, blustering winds made confusion all round. In the end, they conquered Cronos, and bound him in chains, and shut him up in dark Tartaros.

As far as heaven is high above the earth, so deep is Tartaros below the earth. Nine days and nine nights a stone would fall from heaven to earth; nine days and nine nights it would fall from earth to deep Tartaros. A brazen wall runs round it, and brazen gates close it in; there Cronos was in prison, guarded by the Cyclôpês and the three hundred-handed monsters. In front of the gate stands Atlas, immovable, bearing the heavens upon his shoulders. A fearful watch-dog guards the gates, Cerberos, with three heads and three gaping mouths. When anyone goes in, Cerberos fawns upon him, and licks his hands with his three tongues; but if anyone tries to go out, Cerberos devours him up. There Night and Day meet together, and greet one another, as one passes in and the other passes out. Within dwell Sleep and Death, brothers, the children of Night. Sleep can wander over the earth at will, seizing men and letting them go; but Death, once he gets hold of a man, never lets him go again, for there is no pity in his heart.

And there dwells Styx, the lady of the black river of

Hate, eldest daughter of Ocean. When quarrels arise among the immortal gods, then Zeus sends his messenger Iris, with a golden jug, to bring some of the waters of Styx, which falls from a high and beetling rock. The gods must swear an oath by this water. If any of them breaks the oath, for one year he lies breathless, and cannot partake of sweet nectar and ambrosia; after that year he is cut off from the meeting of the gods for nine years more, and then only may he come back and join their company.

In that dark place the banished Titans dwell, guarded by the monsters. And the Cyclôpês are always busy, forging the thunderbolts of Zeus.

After the victory, Zeus and his two brothers were ready to fight each other now, which should be King; but the wise Prometheus persuaded them to cast lots, and to share the sovereignty amongst them. So lots were cast. Zeus became King of Heaven, and Poseidon King of the Sea, and Hadês King of dark Tartaros; but the earth belonged to them all.

III. *Prometheus*

Prometheus, you may remember, was an inventor, and he had filled the earth with animals of his moulding, amongst them Man. He had made Man's body to be like the gods; and into him he put a speck of all the creatures on earth which he had already made, to see what would come of the mixture. There was a speck of the lion, and of the deer, a speck of the cow and of the serpent, a speck of the dog and of the fox, of the monkey and of the owl, the dove and the vulture. It was, indeed, a strange mixture, and so are we still, are we not? Sometimes brave and sometimes timid, now calm and now spiteful, truthful or cunning, mischievous or solemn, gentle or greedy! I have often seen boys very much like monkeys, all but the tail. We need a lot of training before we can get all this chaos into order. Prometheus knew that, and he did his best to train up mankind in the way they should go.

He soon found he could not do much without fire. You remember that fire was a great novelty even to the gods; Zeus got it as a gift from the Cyclôpês; and he soon began to use it for cooking and for making things. He set up one of his sons, named Hephaistos, as the blacksmith and goldsmith by appointment to the heavenly court. Hephaistos also became a builder and architect, and a fine workman he was. So Prometheus, when he saw all these things, understood that he must get fire by hook or by crook. But Zeus did not like the idea at all. When he turned his attention to the earth, and saw all the creatures that Prometheus had been making, he thought them a poor lot. "I will not give fire to such creatures as those," he said. "The earth is a fine place, and it is wasted on them. Let us destroy them, and make a better sort of creatures."

But Prometheus, of course, would not agree to that. Zeus could not do everything, as you must have noticed, and he could not wipe out mankind off-hand. There is a gap in the story here, and we do not know what happened. But it is clear that there was some sort of war, and that Prometheus did his best to protect his friends; for the next thing we hear of is, that Prometheus is making peace between gods and men. They had come to an agreement of some sort, and as usual when a quarrel was made up, there was to be a solemn sacrifice. Some animal was killed, and the gods were to have part of the animal, and men were to have part. In later days, the gods' part used to be burnt, because in that way it could go up to heaven in smoke; but at this time there was no fire on earth, so Zeus came to the place himself to receive his part.

Now Prometheus thought of a way to let his beloved men get the best part. He cut up the victim, and put the titbits into a bladder, and wrapped round it a rough piece of hide. Then he put all the bones together in a bundle, and wrapped round it a layer of fat. He knew Zeus was rather greedy, and had a tooth for fat; so he waited to see what would happen.

When Zeus saw the two parcels, he said, laughing, "Why, my good Titan, this is not a fair division at all. What is that dry old bag?" But Prometheus said, "It is quite fair, sir. We are well satisfied; take your choice, I pray you." As he expected, Zeus chose the enticing parcel of fat. But when he opened it, and saw nothing but bones inside, he was very angry. However, he hid his anger, and pretended he knew about it all the time. "I see this is another of your tricks!" he said. "You are a clever fellow, indeed! Well, never mind." But he had really been taken in, and he did not forget it. He just waited for a chance to pay men out; and when Prometheus begged again for a spark of fire, Zeus flatly refused.

But Prometheus was not to be beaten so easily; and he thought of another trick. He took a long fennel-stalk, and dried it, and cut it in half; and as he passed by the hearth where the fire was always kept burning, he poked the stalk in, and let the pith catch fire inside it. He carried out the stalk, and fastened the other half to it, and left the pith smouldering in the middle. Then he calmly walked out of Olympos, with the fennel-stalk for a walking-stick, and walked down to earth, and nobody noticed anything about it.

Now he had the fire, he began to teach men in earnest. He showed them how to cook, and how to keep themselves warm, how to bake bricks, and burn pottery, how to melt metals and make tools. Men lived no longer in caves and holes in the earth, but made houses to live in. Prometheus taught them how to write, and how to do arithmetic; he taught them about the stars, and gave them medicine to cure their diseases; and they learnt how to tame the horse and the ass and the camel, that these might carry their burdens; and sheep and cows, to give them milk and meat, and to clothe them with skins and fleecy wool.

In fact, he taught them the beginnings of all the arts; and he gave them one blessing above all others. Hitherto they had known the future; they saw trouble and death coming upon them, and they could do nothing to help it, so they were always miserable. But Prometheus took away from men all knowledge of the future; and in its place he put in their hearts blind hopes, which saw nothing, but made them to be always happy. And he gathered together all the evil things that were in the earth, war and quarrel, hatred and greed, pains and diseases, and put them into a large jar; he put a lid on the pot, and sealed it, and gave it to his brother Epimetheus. "Take care of this, my brother," he said, "and never leave it out of your charge. And when I am away, be very careful not to receive any gift from

Zeus. He is man's enemy, and I fear he may try to do him a mischief."

Meanwhile, Zeus had other things to concern him. But when by chance his eye fell upon the earth, what should he see but gleams of fire! How came fire to be on earth? Prometheus must be at the bottom of that! But Prometheus was nowhere to be found; he was busy on earth, as you know. Zeus determined to have his revenge.

So he sent for Hephaistos, the clever craftsman, and told him to make a woman. For there had been only men upon earth so far, and they managed without women as best they could. Hephaistos took a lump of clay and moulded it into the shape of one of the immortal goddesses. He moulded a beautiful creature, like a modest maid; and all the gods and goddesses gave her gifts. The goddess Athena dressed her in fine clothes and taught her spinning, and weaving, and needlework. Aphroditê, goddess of beauty, filled her with grace, and made her such that every man would wish her to be his own. Gold necklaces and bracelets were put upon her, and garlands of flowers crowned her head. Hermês, the crier of the gods, put lovely speech into her mouth, and all sorts of trickery into her mind. They named her Pandora, or All-gifts, because all the gods and goddesses had brought her a gift. Then Zeus sent Hermês to take Pandora down to the earth, and to give her to Epimetheus.

Now Epimetheus was not like his brother Prometheus, who always thought of things beforehand, and looked before he leapt. Epimetheus was a fool, who used to do foolish things first, and afterwards thought, "What a fool I have been!" He was like the man who shut the stable door after the horse was stolen. While Prometheus was busy teaching men, Epimetheus sat at home, taking care of his jar. But when he saw Hermês bringing in this beautiful creature, Pandora, and when Hermês said, "Good day to you! Here is a gift from Zeus, Pandora, to be your wife!" Epimetheus was delighted. He forgot all about his brother's warning, and thanked Hermês, and took the gods' gift, Pandora, with her beautiful voice. She became his wife, and she was the mother of all women upon the earth, who were both a bane and a blessing to men: for they were lovely and charming, and yet they were full of deceit. Of course this was in those early days. They have become better since then, as men have.

It was not long before Pandora began her mischief. She was full of curiosity, and wanted to know about the big jar. "What is in that jar, my husband?" she asked. "You never open it to take out corn, or oil, or anything we use." Epimetheus said, "My dear, that is no business of yours. It belongs to my brother, and he will not have it meddled with." Pandora pretended to be satisfied, but she only waited till Epimetheus was out of the way, and then she went straight to the jar, and took off the lid.

In a moment, out flew a swarm of horrid things, looking like bluebottle flies, and beetles, and wasps, fat and black and ugly, buzzing and darting about everywhere. She clapped on the lid again, but it was too late. They all went flying over the world: plague, pestilence, and all uncharitableness—the evils of the whole world, which the wise Prometheus had shut up safely in the great jar. And that is how mankind has been so unhappy ever since. And when Prometheus came home, and saw what had been done, all that his brother could say was, "What a fool I have been!"

Prometheus himself was cruelly punished for stealing the fire. For Zeus ordered Hephaistos to carry him far away to Mount Caucasos, and there to nail him to a rock, while an eagle came and gnawed at his liver; whatever the eagle ate in the day grew again at night. And there Prometheus was left, until long afterwards he was set free, as you shall hear in due time.

After that Zeus seemed to be content with his revenge. For he made friends with mankind, and men honoured him, and sacrificed to him; and by degrees gods and men came to depend on one another. The gods would have missed men's sacrifices and men's worship; and men looked to the gods for help and the punishment of wrongdoing. Henceforward the histories of gods and men go together.

IV. *Demeter*

You remember that Demeter was one of the family of Cronos; and while Prometheus was amusing himself with making clay models, and Zeus was concerned with getting his kingdom in order, you must not suppose that Demeter was doing nothing at all. She was also interested in the earth, as Prometheus was; indeed, her name means Mother Earth, although she was not the same as the old Mother Earth who was her own mother, and the mother of so many strange monsters. The new Mother Earth, if I may call her so, had now a daughter of her own, called Persephonê, who was very beautiful, and Hadês, the King of Tartaros, fell in love with her, but Demeter would not hear of the match. Persephonê used to live in our world, which had become a beautiful place, full of flowers and fruit, and the songs of birds; she had a number of friends, the daughters of Oceanos, the Ocean, who was himself one of the sons of the old Mother Earth. They used to play about in the fields and groves, and plucked the flowers, singing and dancing together.

Now Zeus was in favor of his brother's wish; and he asked the old Mother Earth to produce a wonderful flower, in order to attract Persephonê to the proper spot where Hadês was to carry her off. There was a meadow in the island of Sicily where all sorts of flowers grew: rose and crocus and violet, iris and hyacinth; and there Mother Earth put forth the best of all, a splendid tuft of narcissus, one hundred blooms upon one stalk, which smelt so sweetly that heaven and earth and sea laughed for joy. The maiden Persephonê put out her hand to take the beautiful flower: but the earth gaped open, and a golden chariot issued forth, drawn by immortal black horses, and driven by King Hadês himself. Out leapt the King, and caught her up, and carried her in his chariot down to his dark kingdom. As he bore her along, she cried loudly for help, but no one heard her cry, except Hecatê, the goddess of the Moon, who heard her voice from her cave; and Helios, the Sun,

21

who saw her from his chariot in the sky; and except her own mother, Demeter, who heard her voice, but saw nothing.

Then Demeter in sorrow sped over land and sea, searching for her daughter; but no man and no bird of course could tell her anything. For nine days she sought her, and found her not; and for nine nights, carrying flaming torches in her hands; but on the tenth dawn she was met by Hecatê, who also bore a torch, and Hecatê said, "I heard her voice, although I saw not where she was, but be sure that Helios, the Sun, who sees all things, must have seen her." So Demeter sped on, until she found Helios; and standing in front of his horse, she said, "Helios, you see everything. Tell me truly of my daughter; for I heard her voice, but saw not where she was."

Helios said, "I pity you, Demeter, and I will tell you. Zeus has done this; he gave her to Hadês, his brother, and Hadês seized her and carried her down to his kingdom in the dark. He is no unfitting husband for your daughter, for he is lord of one-third part of the great universe."

But Demeter was very angry with Zeus, and she would not come to Olympos, but disguised herself and went down among the cities and fields of men. No one knew her, and, in course of time, she came to the town of Eleusis, not far from the city of Athens. There she sat down by the Maidens' Well, where the women of the place used to come for water.

Four maidens, daughters of Celeos, who was chief lord of that place, saw her sitting by the well, like an old woman, tired and travel-stained. One of them said, "Why do you sit here, mother? Come to our house, and you will be welcome."

Demeter said, "I thank you, maidens, and I will tell you my story. My name is Doso, the Giver, and I have now come from Crete, not by my will, for pirates carried me off from my home. They have brought the ship to shore not far off, and while they were all making ready their meal, I slipped away from them, and then I wandered until I came here. Now may you all have what your hearts wish; but tell me of some house where I may go, and do such work as an old woman can do. I am a good nurse, and I can attend a young child, or teach the younger women their work."

One of the maidens answered her, "Mother, what the gods send we must bear; for they are stronger than we. There are many good houses in our town where you could find refuge; but we invite you to our house, where our mother is now nursing her youngest son, but lately born, a child of many prayers. If you can bring him up to be a goodly youth, our mother would give you many gifts, so that other people would envy you. We will go now and tell her." They did so, and returned quickly, running along, to bid the stranger follow. And Demeter followed, with her head veiled, and wearing a dark cloak; and her heart was full of sorrow.

They entered the portico of the house, and there by a pillar they saw the great lady sitting, Metaneira, holding her youngest son to her breast. The girls ran up to her, and Demeter followed; but as she crossed the threshold, she seemed taller to look at, and full of majesty, and Metaneira rose from her couch, and bade her to be seated. But Demeter would not sit upon the couch, to which she was invited; for her heart was too full of sorrow, and she waited until one of the maidens brought her a stool. There she sat, holding her veil before her face. She spoke no word. She would neither eat nor drink, until an old crone made a merry jest; and Demeter laughed for the first time, and felt cheered in heart. Then she accepted a drink, not wine, which she said was not lawful for her, but meal and water mixed with mint in a posset.

Then Metaneira said, "Welcome, lady, for I can see you are no common woman, so full as you are of dignity and grace. But we must all bear what the gods choose to send us. And what I can give you shall be yours in my house. Take this my son, and nurse him for me; and when he grows up to be a big lad I will reward you, so that you shall be the envy of others."

Demeter said, "I accept the charge gladly; there shall be no heedlessness in me. No witchcraft shall touch him, and no gnawing worm, for I know charms that are stronger than worms and witchcraft."

She took the baby, and tended him; and he grew up without food or milk, like something divine. For D would anoint him with the ambrosia of immorta' she would breathe softly upon him as she held hi breast; but at night, unknown to his parents, she would plunge him like a brand into the fire. And they all wondered to see him grow so big and strong; he seemed to be more than a mortal babe. Indeed, Demeter would have made him immortal; but it so happened that Metaneira watched, and saw what she did, and cried out, "Demophon, my son, this strange woman is burying you deep in the fire! What will become of me!"

Demeter was angry when she heard this. She caught up the boy out of the fire, and threw him down on the ground, and cried out:

"What fools you mortals are! You cannot foresee either good or evil. And now you have done a mischief past all healing. I would have made your boy immortal, free from death and old age; but now he must abide his fate, and die when his time comes. Yet he shall have everlasting honour, since he has lain upon my knees, and slept in my arms. For I am that Demeter, whom both gods and men delight in. Now let all the people build me a temple here in Eleusis, and I will teach you my holy rites, to celebrate here for ever."

As she said this, the goddess threw off her aspect of an old woman, beauty spread round about her, and a lovely fragrance was wafted from her robes, and a light shone from her body, and golden hair streamed down over her shoulders, so that the whole house was filled with brightness. And so she went out.

Metaneira remained speechless and amazed, and forgot all about her son, lying on the ground; but he cried pitifully, and his sisters heard him, and ran quickly from their beds. One picked up the baby, and laid him in her bosom; one revived the fire; one looked to their mother: then they gathered about the babe, and washed him; but he was not comforted, for they were less skilful nurses than the goddess.

In the morning they told Celeos what had happened; and he gave orders for a temple to be built, as the goddess had commanded. The temple was built, and there Demeter sat; but she would not be comforted, for she still mourned her lost daughter. She caused a dreadful year for mankind; the seed would not sprout, no fruit would grow, no flowers were to be seen. And famine would have destroyed the whole race of men, out and out; but Zeus observed it, and sent down Iris, the messenger of the gods.

Iris came down to Eleusis, and saw Demeter sitting there in her temple; and she said, "Demeter, I have a message from Zeus, who bids you come to the meeting-place of the gods." But Demeter said, "I will not come"; nor would she move, although Zeus sent each of the gods in turn to call her, and they made her great promises and offered choice gifts. Still, she declared that she would never set foot on Olympos or let the earth bring forth her fruits, until she should see her daughter once again.

Then Zeus sent his herald and crier, Hermês, down to the realms of Hadês in the dark underworld. And he found Hadês reclining upon his couch with Persephonê beside him, his unwilling bride, sad and sorrowful as her mother, and Hermês said, "King Hadês, I am sent by Zeus to bring up Persephonê to the gods, that her mother may see her again; for she threatens to destroy the whole race of men with famine, and then there will be no one to honour the gods and to do them sacrifice."

Hadês smiled grimly when he heard the behest of Zeus; and he said, "Go now, Persephonê, and be kind to me; I am no unfitting husband for you, for I am brother to Father Zeus. And while you are here, you shall rule all that lives and moves, and all shall worship you and pay you due offerings, or he shall be punished." But before she went, he managed to make her eat some pomegranate seed, for he wanted to bring her back again; if she had not eaten, she could have remained with her mother for ever, but she did not know that. Then Hadês brought out the golden chariot and the black horses, and Hermês took the reins, and drove them over land and sea, until they came to Eleusis, where Demeter sat in her temple.

When Demeter saw Persephonê, she ran out, and Persephonê leapt down from the chariot, and they fell into each other's arms. But as she held her daughter, Demeter's heart misgave her, and she said, "Tell me, my daughter, did you taste any food while you were away? If you have not, you may live with me and your father among the immortal gods; but if you have eaten anything in the dark underworld, you must go back there. And how were you carried away?"

Persephonê said, "Mother, when Hermês came to bring me back to you, I sprang up at once for joy; but Hadês put a pomegranate seed into my mouth, and forced me to swallow it against my will. And I was carried off as I plucked a lovely narcissus bloom, while I was playing with my friends."

So they comforted one another: partly in joy and partly in sorrow, for since Persephonê had eaten the pomegranate seed, she was bound to return to the dark world.

Then Hecatê came up, and embraced Persephonê, and from that time Hecatê became her servant and companion.

Then Rheia, the mother of Zeus, came and led Demeter and her daughter into the presence of Zeus. And Zeus promised all honour to Demeter among the immortal gods, and she might have whatever rights she would choose; and Demeter was pacified, and allowed the seed to sprout and the fruits of the earth to grow, and all the flowers of spring blossomed forth again. And she went again to Eleusis, and taught the princes of Eleusis all her secrets. She gave to Triptolemos, the son of Celeos, the seeds of wheat, and sent him in a chariot drawn by winged dragons all over the earth, to teach men ploughing and sowing. She also established a feast in her temple, where the people every four years celebrated great Mysteries, in which they were taught holy doctrines and the laws of good life.

Her daughter Persephonê had eaten in the world below, and she must return there; but Zeus ordained that she should remain there only one-third part of the year, and that for the other two parts of the year she should live with her mother. So for one-third of the year, Persephonê lives underground, and then it is winter, and the leaves fall, and all seems dead upon the earth; but in the springtime, when Persephonê comes up again, the trees put forth leaves, and the flowers bloom, and the kindly fruits of the earth grow up, and men are able to live and be happy.

V. *Athena*

Some of the Greek stories are beautiful, like that which you have just heard about Persephonê. But some stories are wild and savage, because they belong to the early beginnings of Greek religion, which rose out of chaos very much as our world rose out of chaos. Yet these stories, both ugly and beautiful, were all in the minds of the Greeks; and I tell both kinds to you, or else you would know only part of the Greeks. You may see how their religion and their poetry is like the history of mankind itself, which begins in savagery, and rises to something noble and fine. So you must be prepared to hear other childish stories, before you come to learn the thoughts and beliefs of the wisest Greeks.

One such tale is the birth of the goddess Athena, a maiden goddess, who never married a husband, but was like a strong man, clothed in armour and always ready to fight. This is how the birth came about.

Zeus had for his wife Hera, daughter of old Cronos the Titan, as you remember; but he was not content with one wife. Like King Solomon, he had many wives; and one of them, Metis, caused him great anxiety; for Mother Earth told him that if Metis bore a son, that son should be lord of heaven. Zeus accordingly remembered his father Cronos, and what does he do but swallows up his wife whole. Before long he had a bad headache, which got worse and worse until he could bear it no longer. So he sent for Hephaistos, his son, the clever smith, and told him to chop open his head with an axe. "Why, sir," said Hephaistos, "that will kill you!" "Nonsense!" said Zeus, "gods cannot die: chop away!" And Hephaistos raised his axe, and brought it down with a great crash on the head of Zeus, and split it open: and out of the split jumped a little figure, a young goddess it seemed, clad in armour, which rapidly grew bigger until she was full size. As she leapt out, she uttered a loud battle-cry: the heaven shivered, and Mother Earth did quake. The split in the head of Zeus closed up again, and now the headache was quite well. This was the goddess Athena, whom Zeus always loved very much after that. She was daughter of Metis, which name means cleverness, and she came out of the head of Zeus; she was the cleverest of the goddesses, and afterwards taught people how to spin, and weave, and sew, and how to paint and carve, and do all kinds of clever things, better than Prometheus had done.

VI. *The Olympian Household*

And now we have some kind of order in the universe. The three brothers have each his own department, and each his own home. Zeus and his gods live in heaven, that is in the sky, or as the Greeks sometimes said, on Mount Olympos, because that was the highest mountain in Greece, and nearest the sky. The Greeks were rather muddled about this, but it does not really matter. In any case, the gods were called Olympians, and they had a regular court up there, wherever it was; a palace, with apartments or separate houses for the inhabitants, horses and chariots, food and drink, regular hours for meals, and everything very much as it was to be later in a royal palace on earth. Hephaistos was the general craftsman; he had a smithy, where he made wonderful works in gold and silver and bronze, even little chairs that could roll about of themselves. Athena, whose birth you have heard of, soon settled down as court dressmaker, spinning yarn and weaving and sewing and embroidering, like any good housewife. She invented all sorts of arts besides, such as pottery and painting, for she was a clever creature.

The household included the old persons we know, although we do not hear much of most of them. Zeus was there, of course, with his mother Rheia the Titan, and Hera, his wife; Demeter, now she was reconciled again, and Persephonê in the summer; Aphroditê, goddess of love and beauty. Aphroditê was married to Hephaistos, which is surprising, for she was the loveliest creature alive, and he was ugly, and hairy, and swarthy; they must have been like Beauty and the Beast. Hephaistos was not quite equal to the others in rank, for Hera his mother disliked him because he was ugly, and he used to serve the nectar at table. I do not know who did the cooking, but if Olympos was like a good Greek house, the goddesses of the household did it. There were many others connected with this household, who must have been there or at least near by; for it was increasing by the various sons and daughters of Zeus. Hera was the mother of Arês, the god of war, and the goddesses of Youth and Birth, Hêbê and Eileithyia. Another wife of Zeus bore to him the three Horai, or Seasons, named Law, Justice and Peace, and the three Fates, Spinner, Portioner, and Never-turn-back. Another was mother of the three Graces, Brightness, Bloom and Merryheart. Another wife brought him the nine Muses, who loved singing and dancing. There were also a great number of divine beings, not so important as these, who lived in different parts of the universe; they were all related, and all knew each other, wherever they were, but they lived in the country, and did not come regularly to Olympos.

Zeus was the head of the family; and on the whole, he managed his big household with tact. He was an easy-going creature who loved peace and quiet, and he let them alone as long as he could; but sometimes they made such a to-do, he could stand it no longer, and then he would lose his temper, and knock the gods all over the place, for he was very strong. He said to them once:

"Just listen to me: you may try it if you like. Fasten a golden chain to me, and pull on it, all of you, gods and goddesses together, and you will never pull great Zeus down to earth, however hard you may try. But if I choose, I can pull you all up, with earth and sea too, and fasten you to a peak of Olympos, and there in the air you shall all hang."

Hera in particular was a great trial to him. She had a bad temper and a sharp tongue; and once when she had tried him too far he hung her over the edge of heaven by her hands, with a big stone fastened to each foot. On this occasion, her son Hephaistos tried to help her; whereupon Zeus picked him up by the leg, and threw him out of heaven. All day long he fell, and in the evening, down he came plump onto the island of Lemnos. The fall hurt his legs badly, and the people of Lemnos nursed him back to health. After that he had to keep hidden for a long time; in the end he came back to Olympos, but he was always lame, and when he carried the nectar round it was a great joke to laugh at his hobbling gait. But he was a good-humoured creature, and bore no grudge.

VII. *Apollo and Artemis*

One of the quarrels of Hera concerned a maiden of the Titans, named Leto, who was always mild and gentle, kind to both men and gods, gentlest creature in all Olympos. Zeus loved her, because she was so gentle, and made her one of his wives; but Hera was not gentle at all—she was jealous, and vowed that Leto should have no children. She drove Leto out of Olympos, and laid her commands on earth and sea, that no place should give harbourage to Leto. So Leto wandered all over the world distracted, praying every land and every island to help her; but they all refused, for fear of Hera's commands. At last Leto espied an island, floating on the top of the sea, so that it was no part either of sea or land; this was the little island of Delos. Then by the power of Zeus, four pillars of adamant grew up from below sea, and rooted Delos to the bottom of the sea; and there the children of Leto were born, by the side of a beautiful palm-tree.

These children were twins, Apollo and Artemis. A nurse gave them nectar, the drink of the gods, then ambrosia, the food of immortality; and as gods do, the children quickly grew strong and wise, and Apollo cried out:

"I shall ever love music and the bow, and I will declare to men the will of Zeus in truthfulness." And to the amazement of all who saw it, he began to walk upon the earth; and the island of Delos burst into bloom with golden flowers. Artemis also, his twin sister, loved the bow, as Apollo did; she became afterwards great at hunting, and ranged the woods and forests with bow and arrows, attended by a train of nymphs, who were something like the gods, but inferior. Both of them had many temples and many worshippers.

But Apollo, out of all his sacred places, all over the world, on mountain-sides and by the flowing rivers, always loved best of all the little island of Delos, and its little hill, because there he was born; and from the little hill, Cynthos, he took one of his favourite titles, and was called the Cynthian. On this hill is still to be seen his sacred cave, where he was worshipped ever after, until the Greek gods all passed away, and the Christian God took their place. There he had an oracle, giving answers with divine voice to all who sought his aid, the first of many such oracles of Apollo; and there he had great feasts, with splendid processions and ceremonies, with dancing and singing of hymns, and games and sports to amuse the people. Trains of young men and young women sang in honour of Apollo and Artemis, whose arrows bring death and pestilence upon men if they are offended, and punishment upon evil-doers; and these worshippers could imitate the strange languages and chatterings of all the races of men, so that a foreigner would think that his own people were singing.

But I am going on too fast in the story, for as yet Apollo is only a beginner. He has to make his way in the world, and to earn a place in the divine court. And so he became a great traveller and colonizer, seeking everywhere for places where he might settle; and he did not scruple to take possession of a convenient shrine, even if some one was there before him. This is what he did at Delphi, as I shall now explain to you.

He passed over the sea, then, this way and that, sitting upon a tripod, which served him instead of a ship. A tripod is a three-legged stool; and this tripod was a fine one, made all of gold, as was proper for a god, and having two wings where the handles of the tripod usually are: thus it could skim along the surface of the sea, like a flying-fish, and round about it the dolphins leapt out to see what was coming, and dived back again. I cannot tell you all his travels, but I will tell you now how he came to Delphi.

Apollo had already been to report himself in Olympos. We do not know how the gods received him, but I should think they may have been doubtful at first of the stranger, and snubbed him; in any case, he thought he had better look out for a more notable place to settle than the little island of Delos, which Hera sneered at, we may be sure. So he came down from Mount Olympos, and passed over to the great island of Euboea, but found nothing there. Then he crossed the narrow strait which divides Euboea from the mainland, about fifty yards wide, and passed over the place where the city of Thebes was afterwards to be. A few miles from Thebes, he came to a likely place, where was a spring of water, named after the nymph who lived in it, Telphusa. Apollo was pleased with the place, and said, "Telphusa, I think this place will do nicely for me, so I will just build a temple here."

This did not suit Telphusa at all; she wanted to keep her own place for herself, and who was this upstart that he should calmly take possession of it? So she answered, "If I may say so frankly, I do not think you will like this place. Horses and mules are passing by all day long, and they all drink of my water; I am sure the noise of their trampling will disturb you. Besides, the people will be eager to gaze at a well-built chariot, or a well-matched team, and they will not pay proper attention to your temple, where by the way they will be expected to make some offering themselves. But I can tell you the very place—you know best, of course. You see that great mountain, Parnassos, with its peaks covered with snow? In the dell just below it is a place called Crissa, and there is room to build you a fine temple; the path is too narrow for chariots, and you will have none to disturb you, but all those who dwell around will bring you offerings, and seek your help."

Apollo was persuaded, and went on his way, along the lake-side and into the mountain glens, by a path which was to be famous in years to come. As he crossed the summit of the pass, he saw before him a deep valley, with steep rocks on either side, but at the bottom, a water-course, and trees growing thick; at the end of the valley was a wide and fertile plain, full of trees. It was like a river of trees flowing into a sea of trees, and beyond sparkled the real sea in the distance.

When he had come about half-way down towards the plain, he saw the little town of Crissa, and above it a dark cleft in the rock, from which a stream came bubbling out.

There was room for a temple here; but here, also, some one was settled before him. For here was a sacred place of Mother Earth, a hole or cave where gusts of strange vapour came out of the rock, and the place was guarded by a dragon, a great bloated monster, which used to destroy the crops with her breath, and to devour the farmers' cattle and sheep: a terrible and bloodthirsty pest was this dragon. Apollo shot the monster with arrows from his bow; she writhed about, and tried to bite him, but could not, nor could her deadly breath hurt an immortal; so there the dragon died.

And Apollo said, "Rot there, you monster; you shall do no more harm to man." And the dragon rotted; and the place was called Pytho, which means the rotting-place, and Apollo took a title himself from this place and was called Pythian Apollo. For he took possession of the sacred cave, where Mother Earth had her oracle, and of the sacred spring, Castalia. Close by he built his own temple, not very large at first, but it was to grow great by and by: and underneath the temple, in a small chamber cut out of the rock, he made the vapour come up, which had such strange effects on those who breathed it.

Apollo now had a temple, but he had no servants and priests; what was he to do? As he was wondering, he saw from afar—for the gods can see farther than we can—he saw a ship leaving the coast of Crete, full of Cretans. Apollo knew that the Cretans were great men for sacrifices and for laws, and that it was the Cretans who guarded Zeus, the father of Apollo, when Zeus was a baby in the Cretan cave.

Apollo therefore took the form of a dolphin, swiftest of fishes, and he sped through the sea until he reached the Cretan ship: then with a great leap, he shot out of the water, and leapt against the side of the ship, making its timbers quiver and shake. The sailors did not know who he was but they sat still in fear, and kept on their course as it was set, towards the north-west; and by the will of Zeus, a south-east wind blew them quickly forwards. Past the Laconian coast they sped, and on towards the coast of Elis, and when they would have put in to land, the ship would not obey the helm, but Apollo guided it whither he would. And when they came over against the mouth of the Gulf of Corinth, the wind veered to the west, and blew them straight into the little bay which lay by the plain of Crissa.

Then Apollo leapt out from the sea, like a shining star, and sped to his temple; from which he returned in the shape of a handsome young man, with long hair flowing over his shoulders, and he said, "Strangers, who are you?"

They said, "Sir—though you look more like a god than a man—hail to you! Now tell us, what is this place? We are Cretans, and we were bound elsewhere, but some god has brought us here against our will."

Apollo replied, "Strangers from woody Crete, I am Apollo, the son of Zeus; and you have been brought here to keep my rich temple, which shall be honoured among men. Take in your sails, and draw up the ship on the sand, and upon the shore build an altar and sacrifice to Apollo the Dolphin. Then take your meal, and follow me to my temple at Delphi."

They did so, and followed him up the slope, singing the Healer's Hymn, which they had been used to sing in Crete. Then Apollo showed them his temple, and said, "Here you shall abide, and care for my temple; and you will not need to plough the land or to keep herds; for my worshippers will come from far and near, and they will bring many sheep for sacrifice."

He procured priestesses, also, to help in the oracle. In turns they sat on a tripod in the secret cell under the temple; and the priestess, as she drank in the wonderful vapour, became inspired, and uttered strange words in an unknown tongue.

The priests could not interpret the words, nor indeed could Apollo himself; but he know one who could, and that was the ancient god Pan, who lived in Arcadia. And Apollo went to Pan, and learnt from him the art of divining, and taught his priests; so that after that the priests were able to tell the meaning of the words which the priestess uttered, and to answer the questions which the worshippers put to the god.

VIII. *Pan*

Pan was one of the old ancient gods, a strange creature unlike the rest. Some say he was the son of Zeus, but some again say he was the son of Cronos, and I am inclined to think that this is true; for the children of Zeus were all like the gods, even Hephaistos. For although Hephaistos was ugly (so that Hera his mother hated him), he had two arms and two legs, and was clearly one of the divine race; but Pan was half a goat, and that looks like the old generation. It looks like a son of Cronos too; for such another son of Cronos was Cheiron, half man and half horse. Pan was shaggy with hair all over, and he had two short horns on his head; from his waist downwards he was like a goat, with a tail, and his knees turned the wrong way, and he had goat's hooves. Whoever his father was, and whoever was his mother (for that is uncertain too), he was born in Arcadia, among the mountains, and there he dwelt, the friend of the herdsmen and the hunters and the fishermen. He was attended by a troop of servants, like himself, at least in so far that each had a long tail, and some had also goat's feet; these were called Satyrs.

He was fond of all the nymphs of the trees and the springs and the hills, and one of them always attended him, the nymph Echo; so that when he uttered his piercing cry in the forests, high up on the mountain-side Echo would answer him. Pan quite fell in love with Echo, and often chased her about the hills; but he never caught her, for she was always just before him, or just behind him, giving back his cry. The hunters and herdsmen all loved him, but they feared him also, because his loud cry sometimes put a sudden terror into men's hearts, so that they ran away helter-skelter, without knowing why; this they called Pan's terror, or a panic, as we call it still. He would do this even in war, if he chose to help any army of fighting men; and long ages afterwards, he is said to have raised his cry among the Persians at the battle of Marathon, and made the Athenians drive them in rout. Then the Athenians took him into their city of Athens as one of their gods, and gave him a cavern which you can still see on the side of the Acropolis hill.

But that was long after; the time we now speak of was when Apollo was just making his way in the world, and there were no great cities of men as yet. The hunters and the herdsmen, who go up into the mountains in the spring-time, when the Pleiades rise in the sky, and stay there until they set in October, asked his help in tending their herds and hunting their game; and they made him thank-offerings, head and horns or a skin, which they would hang on the branches of some large tree. Pan was fond of music and dancing, and he invented the panspipes, seven hollow reeds of different lengths, giving different notes, which he fixed in a row, with the hollow ends upwards, and played by blowing into them under his lip. You can hear the panspipes if ever you find a Punch-and-Judy show. As Pan played on the pipes, the Satyrs would all dance around; and the hunters and herdsmen imitated him, and danced, and tootled on their pipes. At midday he would sleep, in some shady spot by a spring of water; and the people were very much afraid of disturbing Pan at midday. A Greek poetess, named Anytê, has written this verse about Pan:

> Why in this dark lone forest do you play,
>   O rustic Pan, on a melodious reed?
> That on the dreary hills my heifers may
>   Have pasture, and on bearded grain may feed.

Pan knew all the secrets of the forest and of the earth, for he lived close to Mother Earth; and he had this gift of divining, which he taught to Apollo, as you have heard.

IX. *Hermês*

But the art of divining was not all that Apollo had to learn; he loved music and singing, but he had no instrument to play on, and before you hear how he got one, you must listen to the story of Hermês.

He has already come into this history, but I cannot keep all the things exactly in order as they happened, or the stories would be a collection of bits all mixed up. So now I must tell you how Hermês came to join the company of the gods. Hermês was himself a son of Zeus, and his mother, Maia, lived in a cave on Mount Cyllênê in Arcadia; and there he was born—a marvellous baby! For he was born in the morning, at midday he played on the harp, and in the evening he stole Apollo's cattle. He was to be the prince of tricksters, the cleverest creature in the world, a friend of cattle, a bringer of dreams, a giver of good luck, who could outwit both gods and men. He even made the tortoise sing; and this is the story.

As soon as he was born, and laid in the cradle, he leapt out, and went off in search of Apollo's cattle. Just outside the cave, what should he see but a big tortoise, waddling along. Hermês laughed, and said:

"Here is a sign of good luck, the first thing! Good day to you! I am glad to see you, tortoise; where did you get that dappled shell to cover you with, a fine treasure here in the hills? I will take you inside, and you shall profit me greatly; I will show you the greatest respect. But it is a pity for you that you came out this morning; there is no place like home—it is dangerous out of doors. Alive, you are useful to keep off the witches, but if you die I will teach you to sing."

No sooner said than done. He took the tortoise into the cave. Then he cut off its head and legs, and scooped out all the flesh, and cut away the lower part of the shell; he bored holes in the upper round of the shell, and fixed reeds across the inside, and stretched a piece of skin tight across the hollow part of the shell over the reeds. Then he fixed two horns in the upper part of the shell, and joined their tops by a bridge. Lastly, he tied seven strings of sheep's gut to the bridge, each one a little tighter than the last, and fastened the ends at the bottom of the shell. He touched each string in turn, and each gave a different note, because they were each of different thickness and tightness; then he played tunes, while he sang little ditties, full of mirth and fun.

But his mind was now bent on other things; so he laid his newly made harp in the cradle, and ran out to find something to eat.

He climbed a hill which overlooked a plain where the

cattle of the gods were feeding. Thither he descended, and cut out fifty of the best cows, and drove them to a lonely spot, driving them backwards, that he might spoil the tracks; he tied under his feet bundles of myrtle-twigs, so that they would not make a mark like feet.

On his way, he passed an old man, digging about his vines; and he said, "Old man, I think these vines will bear you a good vintage, and you will make plenty of wine with the fruit, if you can keep a quiet tongue in your head, and remember to forget what you have seen." And on he went, until as night drew to an end, he reached the byres and drinking-toughs by the river Alpheios. There he fed the kine, and gave them drink. And then he gathered a pile of brushwood, and prepared to make fire: for it was Hermês who found out the way to make fire with two sticks. He took a block of dry wood, and a dry stick which he sharpened; then he twisted the point of the stick round and round on the block, until a little sawdust wore out of it, and by and by this grew hot, and at last kindled into flame. And he piled the brushwood into a trench, and set fire to it. If only he had been in the world before, he might have saved some trouble for Prometheus.

Then he threw down two cows, and bent their heads to their flanks, and cut the vital spot. He flayed them, and laid their skins on the rocks; then he cut out the choicest parts, and pierced them with spits, and roasted chine and paunch over the fire. He laid out the meat on flat stones, and divided it into twelve parts as offerings to the twelve great gods; and although he would have liked very much to eat some, being a god he contented himself with the smell. And after that, he burnt up the heads, and hooves, and left no trace of his theft. He threw his foot-gear into the river, and passed quietly back to his cave, where he snuggled down into the cradle, with his beloved harp by his side.

But his mother saw him; and she said, "Naughty rogue! What have you been doing out in the night, clothed in shamelessness as in a garment? I think Apollo will soon have you out of this place, tied up in ropes like the thief that you are. You are born to be a nuisance to gods and men!"

Hermês said, "Mother, why do you scold me as if I

were a feeble babe? No, no, I will make your fortune. Why should we live here in a cave, with no followers and no offerings? We are gods, and we may as well be rich and enjoy life as they do. I will be Apollo's equal, or else I will be prince of robbers. I will break into his great house at Pytho, and take his tripod and his other treasures, see if I don't!"

By this time, as the sun rose, Apollo had gone to the place where his cattle were kept, and he soon missed the stolen cows; so he set out in search of them. Before long he came across the old man, who was then grazing his beast; and he said, "Old man, I am seeking my cattle, fifty fine cows, which have strayed away. Have you seen anyone driving cows?"

The old man said, "Good sir, it's hard to tell all that one's eyes do see. Many travellers pass this way, some honest, and some not, and it is difficult to know one from another. However, I was digging about my vines all day, and I think I saw, but I do not know for certain, I think I saw a child, whoever he was, with some cattle; he had a long stick, and he kept walking from side to side, and driving the cattle backwards, with their heads towards him."

So Apollo went on, and by and by he came on the tracks of the cattle. "Here they are," he said, "turned towards the meadow, it is true; but the other tracks—what can they be? No man or woman can have made them, no wolf or bear or lion. Wonderful tracks they are indeed, each more wonderful than the last!"

And so he followed on, until he came to Cyllênê and the cave; and he went in. But Hermês snuggled down in his cradle, and cuddled himself up in the swaddlings, squeezing head and hands and feet into a ball, and he made as though he were asleep; but he was really wide awake, and held his harp under his armpit. Apollo looked at the mother and child, and opened the chests that lay there, but found nothing. But Apollo knew by his power that the child was the thief; so he said to him:

"Child, confess about the cows, or I will cast you into the darkness of Tartaros, where you will have to be a baby for ever, and you shall be the babies' prince, if you like!"

And Hermês said, "Apollo, what unkind words you

have spoken! Are you looking for cows? I have seen none,
I have heard none, no one has told me anything about
them; I can give you no news, nor earn your reward, if
you offer a reward. Do I look like a cow-lifter? All I care
for is sleep, and milk, and a warm bath. Do not let anyone
hear of this dispute; how surprised the gods will be that a
new-born baby should drive a herd of cows! I was born
yesterday, my feet are soft and the ground is rough; but
if you wish, I will swear a great oath by my father's head
that I did not steal your cows, and I do not know who did,
whatever cows may be; for I never saw one, and have only
heard the word cow."

As he said this, Hermês darted his glances this way and
that, wrinkling his brows, and then he began to whistle
aloud, as if Apollo's talk was just an idle tale. But Apollo
laughed softly, and said to him, "O you little rogue! You
talk so innocently, that I think you must have had good
practice in thieving. I daresay you stripped many a house
last night, and left the poor owners not a stool to
sit on. Many a herdsman will you plague in days to come,
when you have a hankering for meat. But come now: if
you don't want to sleep your last sleep in that cradle,
get out, you comrade of dark night. You shall have the
title Prince of Thieves among the immortal gods."

Then Apollo caught him up in his arms: but the child
gave a loud sneeze, and Apollo dropped him down on
the ground, and said, "Fear not, swaddling-baby, son of
Zeus and Maia. By that omen, I shall find my cattle, sure
enough." Hermês jumped up, and pushed his covering up
to his ear, and said, "Where are you taking me in all this
haste? Is it the loss of your cows that makes you so angry?
I wish all the cows in the world might perish; I don't know
who stole them, and I don't know even what a cow is. Let
us put the case before Zeus, and he shall decide between
us."

For now Hermês saw it was of no use to resist; he
began to walk over the sand, and Apollo came after, and
they climbed up to the top of Mount Olympos, where
Zeus their father holds the scales of judgment. There was
an assembly on that day of the Olympian gods, and the
two stood before the knees of Zeus.

Then Zeus said, "Where do you come from now,

Apollo, driving this rich booty before you? A new-born babe!—but he marches in front like a herald. This must be some weighty matter for us to decide."

And Apollo said, "Sir, it is a weighty matter, although you are pleased to make fun of me, as if I were the only god on the look-out for spoils. Here is a child, a thief and a robber, whom I found on the hill of Cyllênê; never in all my days have I seen one so pert as he is. He stole my cows, and drove them away last evening to Pylos; and wonderful tracks they made; the cows seemed to be going to the place they came from; but he himself strayed all over the place, walking neither on his feet nor on his hands, but somehow, as it seemed, on a lot of twigs. I tracked him over the sand, and when he got upon the hard ground, I found an old man who had noticed him. So when he had shut up the cattle somewhere, he went home and lay down in his cradle in the dark cave. When I found him, he rubbed his eyes, and said, 'I have not seen them, or heard of them, so it is of no use to offer me a reward for the finding.' "

Then Hermês said, pointing his finger at Apollo, "Father, I am a truthful child, I cannot tell a lie. He came to our cave at sunrise, looking for his cows. He brought no witnesses, but violently ordered me to confess, or he would throw me down into Tartaros. For he is strong, and I was only born yesterday, not at all like a cow-lifter. Believe me, I did not drive his cows to the house, I never crossed the threshold; Helios the Sun sees everything, but he never saw that; you know I am not guilty. I swear it by your house! Some day I will punish him for this cruel accusation; but now, help the younger!"

And as he spoke, his eyes kept shooting sidelong glances, to see how they all took it, and he held his clothes tight over his shoulders. But Zeus laughed aloud at the cunning little knave, and said:

"Go now, both of you, and you, Hermês, show where you have hidden the cattle." With these words he bowed his head, and at that sign all must obey. So Hermês led Apollo to the place by the river Alpheios, where he had shut up the cows; and as he drove them out, Apollo saw the two hides lying upon the rocks, and said:

"You crafty rogue, how were you able to flay two

cows, and you a new-born babe? I fear the strength you shall have one day; you will not need long to grow!"

He caught up strong withes, and tried to bind Hermês; but the bonds fell off; and as they struggled, Apollo caught sight of the harp, which Hermês had kept all this time hidden under his armpit. Then he coaxed the child, and at last made him friendly; and Hermês took the harp with his left hand, and with his right he touched each of the strings, which gave out their notes; and Apollo laughed aloud, for the music went to his soul. And Hermês played sweetly upon the harp, and sang to its music in a lovely voice: he sang all the story of the gods, how they came to be out of chaos, each in his turn, and how each received his portion. Then he sang praises of Memory, mother of the nine Muses. And Apollo said:

"That song of yours is worthy fifty cows, and I believe we shall soon settle our quarrel in peace. But tell me, who gave you this wonderful thing? And who taught you to sing? For I vow no one on Olympos has ever heard such singing, or seen such a treasure as this thing. We have our songs, and we have our flutes, but I never cared much for them. Here is a choice of three things at once—mirth, or love, or sleep; they are all in your music. Now sit down, dear boy, and respect the words of your elder. I promise you great fame, both you and your mother; I will make you a leader renowned among the gods; I will give you great gifts."

Hermês understood quite well what Apollo meant; and he said:

"You put your questions well; but I am not jealous, I am quite willing that you should learn my art. You shall learn it this day; I mean to be your friend. Now you know everything, since you are one of the gods' company, and Zeus has given you his oracles, and taught you his laws. So you can easily learn what you please, but since you are determined to play on the harp, then take this as a gift from me: play, and sing, and be merry, bring it in boldly to the feast and the dance, to be a joy by night and by day. He who enquires of this with skill and wisdom, is taught by its sound all things that delight the mind, as he caresses it with gentle friendliness; but he who is ignorant, and enquires of it with violence, to him it chatters vanity and folly. So I give you this harp, noble son of Zeus: and I will be keeper of the roving cattle. Then there is no need for you to be angry, although you are a hard bargainer."

Then Hermês held out the harp; and Apollo took it, and gave to Hermês his whip, and made him keeper of the herds: and ever since, Hermês Eriunios, or All-wool, has been the helper and guardian of herdsmen and shepherds; and he became also the god and patron of all traders, who make bargains together.

So these two, Apollo and Hermês, returned to Olympos in friendship. But Apollo said, "Cunning rogue, I fear you may steal my harp from me, and my bow too. Swear me then a great oath, to do nothing but what will be pleasing to me."

And Hermês nodded his head, like Zeus, and promised never to steal anything that belonged to Apollo, and never to enter his treasury; but Apollo swore always to love Hermês, and none better than Hermês. Then Apollo said, "I will give you a staff of riches, a golden wand, which will keep you safe as long as you do good deeds. But I cannot teach you the art of divining, which I know you wish to possess, though you have only hinted at it. I alone may know the wise counsel of Zeus, and I have sworn him an oath that no other god shall know it, save in so far as he bids me reveal it. As for men, if they come to me guided by birds of true omen, I will tell them the truth, and I will not deceive them; but if any trust to idly chattering birds, and invoke me against my will, wishing to know more than the gods do, it shall be a vain errand, yet their gifts I will take. But there are three ancient sisters, having wings, who fly about feeding on honey, like bees; and when the honey inspires them, they are willing to speak truth, but if they are deprived of it, they speak falsely, and go buzzing round each other. These sisters I give to you; enquire to them, and delight your heart, and teach men to do the same, if you will."

So Zeus, remembering how Hermês came before Apollo like a herald, made Hermês the herald and crier of the gods, with a place in Olympos, and he made him his own particular messenger. With his magical wand he was ordered to lead the ghosts of men down to Hadês; for a touch of it makes the sleeping eyes wake, and the waking eyes close in sleep. He was to preside over all games and contests of men, and to stand in the wrestling-school and the gymnasium, with the title of Hermês-in-the-Ring; he was to be giver of luck, that whenever anyone should find a good thing, he would thank Hermês, and call his find Hermaion, or Hermês' gift. And Hermês was to be lord of birds of omen, and lord of the beasts of the forest and the beasts of the field. He plays no more on the harp, but tootles his tunes on the panspipes, which some even say that he invented.

And Apollo now is ever welcome to the immortals. He plays lovely music upon the harp, and all the Muses together sing as he plays; while the Graces and the Seasons dance, with Harmony and Youth and Aphroditê, holding each other by the wrist. His sister Artemis also joins in the dance, and the other gods listen and look on.

X. *Artemis*

Thus Apollo won a place of welcome in heaven; nor was his sister Artemis slow to make good her footing there.

There are three goddesses in Olympos whose hearts were never touched by Aphroditê, the goddess of love.

One is Hestia, which means the Hearth, eldest born of the children of Cronos, and youngest too: for she was born first by her mother, and swallowed first by her father, so that when he came to disgorge his children, Hestia came forth last. Both Poseidon and Apollo sought to wed her, but she refused outright; and touching the head of Zeus, she swore to remain a maiden all her days. So Zeus gave her a high place in the house, and a rich portion: there she guards the hearth, and tends the fire, like a good housewife; in all the temples of the gods she has a share of honour, and a chief place in all the cities and homes of men, for in every house and in every town hall is a sacred hearth, and the sacred fire was kept burning.

The second is Athena, who cares nothing for love, but delights in war, and in practising all clever arts and crafts, which she taught to men. And the third is Artemis, who loves hunting and archery, and the harp with its dances and songs.

You see Hestia lived the natural life of a woman, such as the eldest daughter has lived in many a household on earth; but the other two were quite out of the way. Athena was like a man, as born of a man's head, all brain, with a man's courage too; but Artemis I think wanted to show that she could do as well as her brother. She was not originally like Apollo: she was not charming like him, and she never dreamt of oracles; but as he used the bow, she used the bow, and they were often linked together in worship. Thus she gained a good share of honour and profit along with her brother.

But they were a pushing pair of young gods, and not easily satisfied. Apollo was not content with taking the oracle of Delphi from old Mother Earth; he actually took over the sun, and Artemis, not to be beaten, took over the moon.

Both sun and moon were already well looked after by those of the old Titan stock, Helios and Selênê. When the universe was being brought into order, you may remember that the sun was taken in charge by Hyperion, the fourth son of Uranos and Mother Earth, who used to drive the sun's chariot from morning to evening, and looked after the horses. Hyperion married Theia, the Divine, a most venerable and radiant goddess, and his children were Eos, Helios and Selênê. He then divided the duties among them: Eos took over the dawn, Helios the sun, and Selênê the moon. Helios used to drive over the sky all day the team of four horses, which were named Fiery, Shiny, Scorcher, and Blazer; and in the evening, when they dipped down into the ocean, a golden boat used to carry them round over the ocean stream behind the earth, so as to be ready for next morning. Helios had temples in every part of Greece, on the tops of the hills; the most famous were on the acropolis of Corinth, and on the Island of Rhodes. How he got that last is a pretty story.

When Zeus and the Immortals were dividing the earth among them, so that each should have his own particular part, they forgot all about the Sun-god, for he was busy about his duties, out of sight, out of mind, and no place was allotted to him. But when he next came to visit Zeus, he said, "Sir, what place have you allotted to me?" Zeus was very much put out. "Why," he said, "we forgot all about you. But never mind, we will cast lots again." "Oh no," said Helios, "pray do not do that. I saw just the place for me, as I was driving high over the sea; down in the depths of the sea was a beautiful island, rising gradually up towards the top. Let the Portioner lift up her hands, and swear an oath that it shall be mine." She did so, and the famous island of Rhodes came up from the depths. Helios took, it for his own, and wedded Rhodos, the nymph of the island, and she bore him three sons, who built them a city each, and divided the island among them. But Apollo, I suppose, did not like another god to dispute his omniscience; and it was Apollo's right alone, he thought, to see everything and to know everything, so he turned out Helios, although none had ever made any complaint as to the way he did his duty.

Selênê, sister of Helios, and like him a Titan, drove a silver chariot with two white horses over the nightly sky, but not every night: she had no light of her own, but borrowed some from her brother. She was a loving creature, and one of the wives of Zeus, but she herself was deeply in love with a man, named Endymion, a beautiful youth whom she saw sleeping upon a mountain. She crept down to him, and kissed him, and there she kept him in perpetual sleep, that she might visit him whenever she wished. Artemis then, not to be outdone by her brother, turned out Selênê, and took over the moon.

But this happened long ages after the time I am now speaking of, near the end of the career of the enterprising twins, Apollo and Artemis. At present Artemis is only beginning her course, and she sought to win her footing in Olympos.

Artemis used to hunt the wild boar, surrounded by a company of maidens who attended her. She was a hard-hearted goddess, and deeply resented any slight or rudeness. Once, for example, a young man named Actaion happened to see her quite by accident, as she was bathing in a pool, and he went away at once; but she turned him into a deer, and his own dogs killed him. Another time, when her sacrifices were forgotten, she sent a large boar into the country-side, which dealt ruin all around; but that belongs to another story, which you shall hear in its place. On the occasion which I am to describe, she turned her hunting to good account.

You remember that Zeus at the beginning of his reign had terrible battles with monsters, which he destroyed; but these were not the only rebellions he had to deal with. Poseidon, lord of the sea, had two sons, named Otos and Ephialtês, who were a remarkable pair of beings. Each year they grew one cubit in breadth, and one fathom in height: so at nine years old, they were fifty-four feet high, and thirteen feet six inches broad; and they thought they were a match for a common sort of god like Zeus. So they determined to conquer Zeus, and to rule the universe themselves. They piled Mount Ossa upon Mount Olympos, and Mount Pelion upon Ossa, and they meant thus to climb up into heaven and turn Zeus out. They caught Arês, the war-god, and shut him up in a brazen pot, with the lid on, where they kept him for thirteen months; but he was rescued by Hermês, and came out quite exhausted. Zeus was pleased with Hermês, because this proved that he had been wise to welcome Hermês into Olympos. But Zeus did not seem to take much notice of the big boys; however, Artemis did, because they were great huntsmen, and she knew all about them and how they grew. She changed herself therefore into the shape of a deer; and one day, when they were hunting, she ran between them. Each threw a spear at her, but she skipped nimbly out of the way; so the spear of Otos pierced Ephialtês, and the spear of Ephialtês pierced Otos, and that was the end of them. I do not know what they might have done if they had lived to grow up.

So Artemis had now shown that she was a person of importance; and she began to spread her worship about the world. Wherever she saw a center of worship with some animal in it, she took possession herself. There were two of them in Crete. One goddess named Britomartis protected the hunters, and one named Dictynna, our Lady of Nets, protected the fishers. Artemis turned them both out, and took possession of their worship and their revenues. In Thrace was another, Bendis, who was a protector of hunters, and she also had something to do with the moon. She used to have a relay-race of men on horseback, carrying torches, which must not go out. In Athens, again, there was a ceremony connected with bears. Once a year all the little girls, at ten years of age, had to dress up in brown clothes, and go into the goddess's temple; and if they did not do that, they would not be allowed to marry when they grew up. They were called the Little She-bears. Artemis took over this temple and the Little Bears, and she did the same for Bendis and her torch-race. She even went over to Asia, and she did not despise the ugliest goddess in the whole world, who had a great temple at Ephesus. This was the goddess about whom St. Luke wrote, when he described how the people all cried out for the space of two hours, "Great is Diana of the Ephesians!" For Diana was the Roman name for Artemis.

She also took to herself the worship of Hecatê. You remember Hecatê, who used to attend upon Persephonê, she who met Demeter on her search and carried two torches. Hecatê was a night-goddess, who had something to do with the moon, and knew all about witches. She helped to bring children into the world, and presided over funerals when men died. Artemis took over all Hecatê's work, and the result was, she was thought to be three goddesses in one, Persephonê, Artemis, and the Moon. So her statue often had three heads on one body; it was set up at the cross-roads, and people used to drop cakes and nuts and such things by her statue, for anyone to eat; they called it Hecatê's dinner.

PART 2

XI. *The Flood*

You have heard how Zeus by degrees put his kingdom in order, and made the beginning of law in Olympos. There he held a court of justice, and heard pleadings, and gave his decision according to his laws. These laws were so far the decision of his will, from which there was no appeal. When Zeus bowed his head, all must obey. He demanded an oath by the river Styx, and there were penalties for falsehood. And he was beginning to make his will felt among men; they also had their oaths and their beginnings of justice, their compacts and their sacrifices; and they worshipped the gods, who could not do without the gifts and the burnt-offerings of men, for although they were nourished upon nectar and ambrosia, still the odour of burnt sacrifice, rising in the smoke, was pleasant to them, and they seemed to have got more than pleasure from it somehow. The gods, however, used to travel amongst men; they shared the feasts and the life of men, if they were pleased with them, and often in the shape of beggars and strangers, they watched to see who did good and who did evil. And when men did evil they were punished; sometimes in this world, especially in matters of blood-shed, when the Furies chased the guilty until he was purified; and after death there was also a judgment, of which you will hear by and by. So you will see that gods and men were all mixed up together.

But we cannot sort out all these things into their proper time; gods and men were both growing up side by side, and my stories of the two societies overlap now and then. Prometheus, as you know, was the great friend of man, and he gave him fire, and he taught him everything; but

49

Zeus came to take interest in man more and more, as he became educated himself, and wiser with experience. Once, you remember, he desired to destroy man altogether, and make a new creature to put in his place; and once, but at what time exactly we do not know, he nearly did destroy mankind. For he sent a great flood upon the world, which drowned everyone that it came near. This is how it came about.

We are told that there were Four Ages of Man, of which the first was the best. I suppose that was when all the miseries of mankind were shut up in a jar, and kept safe by Epimetheus, before women came into the world with Pandora, who let out all our troubles by taking off the lid from the jar. The first was the Golden Age, called also the Age of Cronos, before the reign of Zeus began. If Cronos was a savage himself, at least he had sense enough to leave Prometheus alone; and the Golden Age ought rather to be called the Age of Prometheus, I think. In the Golden Age it was very much like the Garden of Eden. Men lived like the gods, free from sorrow and free from disease. They feasted and made merry so long as they lived; they had no hard work to do, for the earth brought forth her kindly fruits without tillage, so that cabbages and lettuces grew like weeds, and men were content with acorns from the oak, or fruit from the trees, or such things as came out of the ground. They had no disease, and never grew old; but when they came to the limit of their days, death came upon them in their sleep and they passed away in peace.

Nor did death end them; for their spirits dwelt on the earth, and still do so, watching and helping mortal man. They are clothed in mist, and seen of none, but they see all the doings of man, whether they be good or evil.

After this generation of men had passed away, came the Silver Age, less noble than the first in body and spirit. For a hundred years they lived like children; then for a short time they lived in foolishness and wickedness, and neglected to worship the gods, and then they perished.

When these came to an end, a third generation came up called the Age of Brass, terrible and strong. They built houses of brass, and made armour and weapons of brass, and tilled the earth with brazen tools, for there was no iron as yet. The men of this race fought together, and perished by their own hands. But in amongst them there grew up another race, half gods and half men, called the heroes, of whom there are many stories yet to tell. The best of the human race are descended from them.

And when the men of brass had perished by their own hands, there came a fourth race upon the earth in the Iron Age, which still goes on. Iron is their metal, and they make tools and armour of iron; they never cease to toil and labour day or night, and they never cease fighting with one another. The father does not agree with his children, nor the children with their father, nor guest with host, nor comrade with comrade. Sons do not repay their parents for their love and care; promises are broken, and evil-doers are honoured. This race also will come to an end, and all that is evil in it will perish utterly; but the good will have their reward.

Now in this Iron Age, Zeus visited the earth, to see whether men were as bad as they were said to be; and he came to the realm of one Lycaon, who was King in Arcadia. Lycaon laughed, on hearing that Zeus had come, and said, "Now then, let us see if he is really a god!" So he killed an innocent man, a hostage in fact, whom he was bound to protect, and cooked his flesh, and set it before Zeus his guest, to see if he would eat it. But Zeus struck the King's house with a thunderbolt, and Lycaon fled terrified to the hills. His rough coat changed into bristling hairs all over his body; he tried to shout, and out came a snarl: for he had turned into a wolf, destined to delight in blood all the rest of his days.

Zeus called a council of the gods, and told them what had been done; and then he declared that he thought it best to destroy mankind. The others said, "But what shall we do? There will be no one to offer sacrifices to the gods." "Never mind for that," said Zeus. "I will provide." The question then came, whether he should launch his thunderbolts on the world, and set it afire; but Zeus was afraid that so great a conflagration might rise to the upper air, and set that also on fire, so that the Olympians themselves would be burnt up.

It seemed best therefore to use water. The winds were bidden to gather the clouds; the rains descended and the floods came, and overwhelmed the whole country of Greece, so that all who dwelt there were drowned; men and beasts, wolves and sheep, lions and tigers, were carried down to the sea, and seals and dolphins swam about in the forests.

But one solitary pair remained: Deucalion, a son of Prometheus, and his wife, Pyrrha, the daughter of Epimetheus. They were good people both, no one more just and no one more strict in worshipping the gods. They had got into a little chest or ark, which was in the house, and the waters carried them to the slopes of Mount Parnassos, close to the cleft where Mother Earth had an oracle; the shrine at that time was in charge of Themis, goddess of Justice, for Apollo had not yet come that way. They gave thanks to Themis, and prayed to the nymphs of that place. When Zeus saw that this innocent pair had been saved, he told Poseidon to recall his floods; and Poseidon bade his trumpeter Triton sound the recall. Triton blew a blast into his hollow shell, and the waves were stayed. Then Zeus made a great hole in the earth, and the waters all ran down, and the land began to appear. For thousand of years, this hole used to be shown in the sacred place of Olympia.

Deucalion looked around on the world, all shining with mud, and said to Pyrrha, "My wife, see, we are the whole population of the world! And the clouds are still dark above us. What should I do, if I were alone—or you, without me? Let us ask what is the will of God."

So they entered the shrine of Themis, and said, "Themis, if the anger of Zeus is satisfied, tell us how to recover the human race." And Themis said, "Go down to the plain, and cover your heads with a veil, and throw behind you your mother's bones."

They went out, and Pyrrha said to her husband, "I am afraid, my dear husband: how can we find our mother's bones? And if we could find them, would it not be wicked to disturb them?"

But Deucalion was not his father's son for nothing; he had some of his father's wisdom, and he replied, "Wife, the gods often speak in riddles. I think Themis means the bones of Mother Earth, that is, stones: let us try them—it can do no harm to try."

Then they veiled their heads, and each of them picked

up stones, and threw them behind their backs. Perhaps you will hardly believe it, but the stones as they fell took on human shapes; Deucalion's became men, and Pyrrha's became women. Even now we show traces of this origin; for we have veins in our bodies, like the veins in a piece of marble, both called by the same name; and men are called peoples, because they grew out of pebbles.

XII. *Athena and Poseidon*

As men multiplied upon the earth, and built cities, they built also temples to the gods. Generally each place had a chief god, which it honoured more than the rest, and we do not always know why they were chosen. Not all the gods pushed their way in like Apollo and Artemis; but there was some rivalry between them, naturally enough. Poseidon was god of the sea, so he did not find it as easy as the others to get places on the land. He got Corinth without much difficulty, because Corinth lay between two seas, and depended for her wealth on the sea. He also wanted Athens; and you might have thought that very proper, because in later years Athens was the great sea-power of Greece, but in the early days Athens did not think much about the sea. Athens lay three miles from the shore, and had no harbour then.

Athena also wanted Athens, and they were told to decide it by giving a gift to mankind: whichever gave the best gift should win. You see how far we have come from the time when Zeus would not give men fire, and only Prometheus gave them anything good! The gods thought of men more kindly now.

So they came to the contest, on the Acropolis hill. Poseidon struck his trident upon the rock—you may still see the cleft it made, under the porch of an old temple: and out sprang a horse. Poseidon was a great god for horses, and in later times, he held famous horse-races. The sea is full of horses, you know, and you can observe their white manes all over it, as they leap about in stormy weather. That was indeed a noble gift to man. It is true, they had horses already, as you heard in the story of Prometheus;

but this was a noble breed, like the Arab, better than their heavy horses with big heads.

Athena came with a little olive tree, which she planted in a garden close by the place where Poseidon struck. I do not think this tree had been known before; it was a new gift, all her own. It is said to have come from the paradise Beyond the North Wind. The tree was adjudged to be the best gift, and the King chose Athena for the chief goddess of Athens, and named the city after her. And it was a wise choice. For the olive became the great wealth of Athens; it fed the people with its fruit, as it does to this day, and it provided a soft and precious oil for their use, to put in their food, and to rub their bodies with when they were tired. They planted the tree everywhere, and made oil for other people to buy, and so they became rich.

Athena's temple at Athens became the most lovely of all Greek temples, and you may still see it, lovely even in ruins. I want you to remember this temple, because it will come into the very last part of our history.

Just before this, the island of Rhodes had come up out of the sea, as you may remember, and the sons of Helios were building new cities there. The men of one of these cities, Lindos, thought they would like their great goddess to be Athena, who had lately sprung out of the head of Zeus, to the amazement of all the world. The new goddess would suit the new island. They hoped to be first in the field, before anyone else could come in. Helios agreed. "But be careful," he said. "Do not waste time; build up an altar at once, and make a sacrifice, and you will have the first claim."

The Athenians were also trying hard, and it was a near thing. In fact, the Lindians got ready their altar first, and the sacrifice, but they were in such a hurry, that they forgot to bring fire up the hill. So they had to make a fireless sacrifice. The Athenians were second in time, but they had fire and everything necessary, so that the smoke might rise to Olympos. Therefore Athena made Athens her chief seat. But she was pleased also with Lindos, and sorry for the hard luck of that place. Zeus sent a shower of gold to fall upon Lindos; and Athena taught them to be the cleverest workers in metal of all the world.

XIII. *The Heroes: Heraclês*

Gods and men had another fight before them, this time as allies; but before we come to that, I must tell you about the Heroes, who came up in the world, as you remember, at some time in man's history. They were half god and half man. The gods were always mixing with men. They had to visit their temples, and receive worship and sacrifice, and they had also to travel about and see how men were behaving; and it often happened that one of the gods would fall in love with a beautiful maiden among mankind, and they would wed with these maidens, and their children were the Heroes. These Heroes lived in the world among mankind, and did many wonderful deeds, but they were not immortal; their bodies died, and after death they were worshipped on earth, but their souls lived still, and some went to the Islands of the Blest, while some were even caught up into heaven.

The greatest of all the Heroes was Heraclês. He was the son of Zeus and Alcmenê, princess of Thebes, and there was great excitement over his birth. Hera was jealous and angry; and as soon as he was born, with his twin-brother Iphiclês, she sent two large serpents into the chamber, to kill the babies. But Heraclês lifted up his head, and clutched the throats of the two serpents, and held them writhing until their lives were throttled out of them. Up jumped his mother, and ran to help, and all the women shrieked out, "He's dead!" In came the men, clad in full armour, in came prince Amphitryon, holding a drawn sword in his hand. When he saw the baby Heraclês, with a serpent hanging limp from each hand, he cried out, "Who told me the baby was dead? It is the serpents that are dead!" But glad as he was, there was something about it which he could not understand; so he went to find old Teiresias, the Theban seer, who lived next door. "Come out, neighbour!" he said, "what does this mean?" And Teiresias told him by prophecy the mighty deeds which the baby was destined to do when he grew up. "And now," he went on, "gather up twigs of briar and wild pear, and with these burn the bodies

of these two serpents; and let some one take up the ashes,
and throw them into the river, and return without looking
behind him; then the river shall carry them out of your
country into the sea."

So Heraclês grew up; and the best masters taught him
to shoot arrows from the bow, and to box, and wrestle,
and fight in every manner, and to read and write, to sing
and to play upon the harp. Prince Amphitryon taught him
to drive the chariot, and Castor himself, the horseman god,
taught him how to manage a horse, and to use the sword
and the javelin, and to fight in armour, and how to lead
men in time of war.

So he grew up till his eighteenth year, and then a sur-
prising thing happened. He was thinking what his future life
was likely to be; probably he had heard something of the
prophecies of Teiresias, and perhaps he shrank from the
danger a little. But he saw, or he thought he saw, two
women approaching him. And one of them ran in front, to
get the first word; and he saw that she was tall and hand-
some, and decked out in gay finery, with her cheeks rather
too red to be natural; and she said to him, "Young man, I
see you are in doubt what to do, and what path of life to
follow. I invite you to follow me; you shall have the easiest
and pleasantest life in the world, no hard work and no
dangers; you shall eat, drink, and be merry, others shall
work and you shall have the enjoyment, and you shall be
as happy as the day is long." And Heraclês said, "What is
your name?" The woman answered, "My real name is
Pleasure, but my enemies call me Vice."

By this time, the second woman had come up. Heraclês
saw this one also to be tall and handsome, but after a dif-
ferent fashion; for she was stately and dignified, and of a
noble look; her dress was all white, truth was in her eyes,
and modesty in her manners. She said, "Young sir, I know
your parents and your breeding, and how you have been
educated and brought up; which makes me hope that you
will be a good workman of noble deeds. I will not deceive
you with promises of pleasant things, but I will tell you the
truth. Nothing that is really good can be got without labour
and hardship, for so the gods have ordained. If you wish
to enjoy the fruits of the earth, you must plough and sow,
and reap and mow. So if you wish your body to be strong,

you must make your body the servant to your mind, and fear not labour and sweat. And just in the same way, if you wish for the gods favour, you must serve the gods; if you wish for the love of friends, you must do good to your friends; if you wish for honour from your city or your native land, you must work for their benefit, and you must defend them from enemies without and tyrants within. Follow me, and I can make you great, and truly happy." Heraclês said, "And what is your name?" She answered, "My name is Virtue."

Then Pleasure said, "See, Heraclês, what a hard road she puts before you! Not a scrap of pleasure in it!" But Virtue said, "Such pleasure as hers leads only to surfeit and weariness; he that tries to be happy, never succeeds; but he that does noble deeds gains happiness without trying."

And Heraclês resolved to follow the hard road, and to put away from his mind the craving for pleasure.

So Heraclês made his choice. But his first task was to master himself, before he could do great deeds with his own strength; for he had a violent temper. And so once he quarrelled with his music-master, who found fault with him, and struck him; then Heraclês lifted up his harp, and struck the man down, and killed him. He was not found guilty of murder, since the other had struck first, but Prince Amphitryon sent him to work on the cattle-farm, that he might school himself and master his temper. While he was there a lion came down from the hills and attacked the cattle; but Heraclês killed the lion, called the Lion of Cithairon, which was the name of the hill country whence he came.

After this he gathered together the young men of the city of Thebes, and they fought against a neighbouring King who held Thebes under tribute, and set Thebes free from the tribute; for which the King of Thebes, whose name was Creon, gave Heraclês his daughter Megara for a wife.

But soon after this a terrible misfortune happened to Heraclês; for madness came upon him, sent by the goddess Hera, who was always his enemy: and Heraclês in his madness killed his own children. When he recovered, he sought how he might atone for his deed, and asked the oracle at Delphi what he should do. The oracle told him that he must live at Tiryns, an ancient city in South Greece, and for years he must serve Eurystheus, King of Mycenai, and do what he commanded. Each year therefore Eurystheus set him a hard task to do, and these are called the Twelve Labours of Heraclês.

(1) The First Labour was the Nemean Lion. There was a terrible lion that ranged on the mountains not far from Tiryns. You should look up this country on the map, for it comes often into the stories of Greece. There is a fertile plain on the east side of Greece, looking towards Asia, which contained three ancient cities, built in the beginning of time by great warriors who came from Asia. Near the coast is the first, Tiryns, and you may see the ruins there to this day; for it was built of huge stones, and every one who sees it is amazed. In the middle of the plain is a large rock, and upon this the second city was built, named Argos; and at the end of the plain is the third city, Mycenai, which is also to be seen still, in ruins, with a wonderful gate, built of huge stones, called the Lion Gate, because above it are the figures of two lions rampant. The whole plain is called the plain of Argos.

Now at Mycenai the hills and mountains begin; and a few miles from it is the valley of Nemea, where this lion of Nemea used to range about. This lion was of huge size; he was a son of the monster Typhon, whom we shall hear of soon; and he could not be wounded with iron, or bronze, or stone. He had a den in one of the rocks, a long tunnel with two openings, where he used to live; and if he were chased he ran into one end, and ran out of the other. Eurystheus commanded Heraclês to bring him the skin of this lion.

So Heraclês took with him his bow, and a quiver full of arrows, and a heavy club which he used to carry. When he came to the place, he could find no tracks, nor could he ask news from anyone, for all the people were afraid to come out and there was no one in the fields. Towards evening, the lion came to his den full fed, with his mouth and chest all spotted with blood, and licking his chops. Heraclês hid by the way, and let fly a shaft at him; but the arrow slid off his skin, for he could not be wounded by iron, or bronze, or stone. Heraclês shot him again, full in the chest, but the arrow fell useless to the ground. The lion rolled his eyes, and saw Heraclês; then lashing his flanks with his tail, he gathered himself up for a spring. As he leapt, Heraclês held up his left arm wrapt in his cloak, and brought down his club with a bang on the lion's head; the club splintered in fragments, but it checked the spring, and the lion stood wagging his head and dizzy with the blow. Then Heraclês threw down his bow and arrows, and leapt on the lion's back, treading down the lion's hind-legs with his own feet, while he put his hands round the lion's neck, and pulled up one foreleg; then he got this leg under his arm, and gripped the lion's throat with his two hands, and bending him backwards, throttled him.

There lay the lion dead on the ground; but how could Heraclês skin him? No iron could cut the skin, no bronze, and no stone: but a thought came into his mind, that he should cut off the skin of the lion with the lion's own claws. And so he did. He brought back the skin to Eurystheus, but he would not give it up; and ever after that he wore that skin as a garment, with the forepaws over his shoulder, and the head like a helmet over his own head, which looked out of the lion's jaws. This is what you always see in the pictures of Heraclês.

(2) The Second Labour was the Lernaean Hydra. There was a marsh in the plain of Argos called Lerna, and in it there was a huge serpent with nine heads, called Hydra the Watersnake, because she lived in the marsh; and her middle head was immortal. Some say she had a hundred heads, and it is difficult to say how many there were—you will soon hear why. Heraclês was commanded to kill this Hydra; so off he went in a chariot, driven by his charioteer, Ioläos, his nephew. When they came to the place, Heraclês jumped out, and shot the serpent with his arrows, but she did not seem to mind that; then he attacked her with his club, but she did not mind that; then he took a sickle, and cut off head after head, but whenever he cut off one head, two grew in its place.

As he was cutting away, he felt a nip on his leg, and what should he see but an enormous crab come to help his friend the serpent. "That is not fair, two to one!" said Heraclês. "Ioläos, come and help me!" So Ioläos came with another sickle, but that only made matters worse. Suddenly Heraclês had a happy thought. "Get me some sticks," he said, "and burn the place!" Ioläos made a fire, and brought up the brands; and as Heraclês cut off a head, Ioläos burnt the place so that new ones could not grow. Then Heraclês cut off the immortal head, and buried it under a rock; and if it has not been moved, I suppose it is there still. In any case, the marsh is there still, and it still breeds a lot of ugly snakes. The crab was killed too, and actually became a constellation in the sky, but I really cannot see why. From this a proverb grew up in Greece,

Even Heraclês is done,
In a fight of two to one.

Heraclês kept the bile of the serpent to dip his arrows in, and thus a wound from his arrows brought death with it.

(3) The Third Labour was the Arcadian Deer. This was a doe, but nevertheless she had antlers, golden antlers and brazen feet, and she wandered all over Arcadia free, for she was sacred to Artemis. Why that was so is another story which I cannot tell you now, for there are so many stories in Greece that there is no end to them. Heraclês chased the doe for a whole year; and we do not know quite how he caught her, for some say it was in a net, and some say he found her asleep. But in the end, catch her he did, and brought her home on his back. On the way, Artemis met him, and wanted to know what he was doing with her doe. She was very angry, but Heraclês said, "I can't help it: Zeus commands me to obey Eurystheus, and Eurystheus commands me to bring him this doe. So what can I do?" Thus he managed to make peace with Artemis, and brought the doe to his tyrannical master.

(4) The Fourth Labour was the Erymanthian Boar. Like the Lion and the Hydra, this boar was a nuisance to the country-side, where it destroyed cattle and crops, and attacked the people who lived there. Eurystheus told him this time, that he must bring in the boar alive; which seems to be just spiteful, since Heraclês had done the other tasks so well. He had to be careful, you see, not to use too much strength, or too little; for if he used too much, he would kill the boar, and if he used too little, the boar might kill him, or at least damage him.

He set out then, and on his way he passed through the country of the Centaurs. These were monsters, you remem-

ber, half horse and half man; they had a man's head and
shoulders, and a horse's body; some were a whole man,
legs and all, with half a horse growing out behind. They
were as swift as a horse, and as strong as a wild beast, and
as wise as men. One of them, named Pholos, had a cask
of wine; and he said, when he saw Heraclês, "Come into
my cave, sir, and let me entertain you; I have a fine drink
here which I have been keeping specially for your visit."
Heraclês thanked him, and came in; Pholos set cooked
meat before him, but he ate his own meat raw.

Then the cask was opened. The wine was a hundred
years old. It was indeed a delicious drink, which Heraclês
had never tasted before; and it spread abroad such a deli-
cious scent, that the neighbourhood became full of it, and
the other Centaurs smelt it, and galloped up to Pholos's
cave, to see what it was. When they saw what it was, they
crowded into the cave, and began to drink it, which made
them wilder than ever.

Now Pholos was frightened, and ran to hide himself,
leaving Heraclês to face the furious monsters. They tore
up trees by the roots to attack him, and threw great stones
at him, and some even picked up axes to cut him down,
or drove at him with firebrands. Their mother, the Cloud,
helped them by pouring about them a thick mist, which did
little hindrance to the beasts with four legs, but made it
difficult not to slip for Heraclês with only two. Yet he was
a match for them; he did not even need help this time, and
so perhaps he had learnt something from his fight with the
Hydra. He killed a large number, and the rest he drove
away. Among the killed Centaurs were Horsey and Hilley
and Blackmane, Hit-for-hit, Thumper, and Bristler. Pholos
came back when the fight was over, and looking at the dead
bodies, he pulled out one of the arrows. "How strange," he
said, "that a little thing like that could kill such great crea-
tures!" and he dropped it down on the ground; but in drop-
ping, the point scratched his foot, and as the arrow was
poisoned, Pholos died too.

After this, Heraclês went on in search of the boar; and he
chased him about in the snow, until the boar fell ex-
hausted in a thicket. Then Heraclês heaved the boar up
on his shoulders, and carried it back to Eurystheus. He
marched into the hall, where Eurystheus was sitting, and

made as though to throw down the boar at his feet; but Eurystheus, who was a coward himself, became terrified at the sight, and ran away, until he saw a large wine-jar buried in the ground with the neck open; into this jar he jumped to hide himself. The boar did no mischief to Eurystheus, but Eurystheus went on to find more labours for Heraclês.

(5) The Fifth Labour was to clean the stables of Augeas. This Augeas was King of Elis: he had thirty thousand cattle, and their stables had not been cleaned for thirty years; but Heraclês was commanded to clean them in one day. He offered to clean them out if Augeas would give him one-tenth of the cattle, and Augeas agreed. Then Heraclês made gaps in the walls of the stables, one at each end, and turned the course of two rivers towards the upper end; the water ran in at the upper end and ran out at the lower end, carrying all the dirt with it. Augeas, however, made an excuse to avoid paying what he had promised. Heraclês punished King Augeas afterwards, for he killed him, and carried off the spoil of the country; and with this spoil he founded the great games at Olympia.

(6) The Sixth Labour was to destroy the Stymphalian Birds. These birds had brazen claws, and brazen wings, and brazen beaks; they used to shoot out their brazen feathers like arrows, and kill people with them, and then they ate their bodies. The birds were gathered about Lake Stymphalos in Arcadia; thence they flew out in swarms, and settled on the fields, and devoured all the crops. Heraclês saw that he could not kill all these birds; but Athena came to his help, and gave him a huge rattle of brass. Heraclês rattled and made a great noise, and the birds rose up; he shot his arrows, and killed some, and the rest flew away. What became of most of them I do not know, but we shall hear of some of them later. At least the Stymphalian Lake and the land of Arcadia were quite cleared.

(7) The Seventh Labour was the Cretan Bull. This was a wonderful and beautiful bull, belonging to King Minos of Crete, which had gone mad. Heraclês caught this bull, and carried him on his shoulders to King Eurystheus; then he let the bull loose again, and the bull wandered all over Greece, and did damage everywhere, until he came to Marathon; and at Marathon he remained, but we shall hear of him also again.

(8) The Eighth Labour was to capture the Mares of Diomêdês. This man was a savage King of Thrace; he kept his mares fastened with iron chains to mangers of brass, and he used to feed them with the flesh of men. Heraclês called for volunteers to help him; and they went to Thrace and attacked Diomêdês, and gave him to his own mares to eat. The mares then became quiet and tame, and Heraclês easily brought them to Eurystheus.

(9) The Ninth Labour was the Girdle of the Queen of the Amazons. The Amazons were a tribe of women, who fought on horseback like men; and their Queen Hippolyta had a splendid girdle. Heraclês led another body of volunteers against these. When he came to their country, which was in Asia Minor, he demanded the girdle, and Hippolyta came to him quite ready to give it; but the other Amazons thought their Queen was being made prisoner, so they attacked Heraclês and his companions. There was a battle, and the Amazons were defeated, and Heraclês brought the girdle back.

(10) The Tenth Labour was the Oxen of Geryonês. This was a horrid monster with three bodies joined at the waist, who lived in an island off the coast of Spain. His oxen were guarded by another monster, and by a dog with two heads. This was a tremendous journey for Heraclês; you see he had been to the far east, and to the north, and now he went to the west, traversing the north part of Africa. Wherever he went, he cleared the country of wild beasts and serpents, and punished lawless men; for as you remember from the story of his youth, all his life was given to the service of mankind, and he did all his great works without payment.

When he came to the Straits of Gibraltar, he set up two pillars, one on each side, to mark the extreme limit of travel; for the sea and the countries outside the straits were unknown in these early days. These were called, ever afterwards, the Pillars of Heraclês (or Herculês).

He then attacked the two-headed dog, and killed it with his club, after which he killed the guardian monster, and shot the three-bodied monster Geryonês with his arrows, and drove the cattle back by land, clearing out the wild beasts on his way, and settling the people in orderly government.

(11) The Eleventh Labour was to fetch the Golden Apples of the Hesperidês. This task was more difficult than usual, because he did not know where they were. So he hunted for them all over the world, and in the course of his journey he had many adventures; amongst them he came to the place where Prometheus was nailed to the rock. Heraclês was angry at the fate of Prometheus; so he set him free, and persuaded Zeus to be kind to him again, and to receive him into the company of Olympos. Prometheus advised Heraclês to find Atlas, his brother, and to ask him where the apples were. For Atlas was the father of the maidens called the Hesperidês, and they had a garden in the far west, in Spain, where they guarded the golden apples with the help of a dragon.

You remember old Atlas, the Titan, who bore up the heavens upon his shoulders. Herclês accordingly sought him out, and asked him kindly to show the way to the Garden of the Hesperidês, that he might get the golden apples. Atlas said, "I must not do that, but I will tell you what I will do: I will fetch the apples for you, if you will just hold up the heavens a bit. But I do not think you are strong enough for that." "Not strong enough!" said Heraclês, "I will soon show you." So he stood by Atlas, and Atlas carefully shifted the weight of the heavens upon his head, and Heraclês held it up with his hands.

It was terribly heavy, much worse than he expected; some of the stars fell out as he held it, because he was new to the job, and very glad he was when he saw Atlas coming back. "Here you are," said Atlas, showing him the apples. "What do you want them for?" Heraclês said. "To give to Eurystheus?" Then Atlas said, "I can do that, it is no trouble at all," and began to go off. You see, he thought it a great piece of luck that some one had come to relieve him of his job. And Heraclês saw that he was in for it, if he was not careful. No doubt his talk with Prometheus had sharpened his wits, for he did not show anger or apprehension, whatever he felt; but all he said was, "I thank you. I am much obliged, but just give me a little help first. I am not used to this weight, and it is rather uncomfortable; hold it a minute while I make a pad for my head." Atlas was not clever, like his brother Prometheus, who had all the brains of the family; he was a stupid thing like his uncle Cronos: so he agreed at once, and laid the apples down on the ground. Then Heraclês thanked him, and shifted the heavens upon Atlas's shoulders again, and picked up the apples, and went off to Eurystheus. I do not know what Atlas said. The heavens have not fallen down yet, so we may suppose the old Titan still does his duty: but we shall see.

(12) The Last Labour was to fetch up the dog Cerberos from Tartaros. There is a dark cave in Mount Tainaron, which is the entrance to Tartaros, and a dark tunnel downwards; and by this way Heraclês went down. He had some adventures in the lower world which you will hear of later; and Hadês allowed him to take Cerberos, if he could do so without using his weapons. Heraclês therefore seized the dog with his hands, and crushed him tight until his spirit was tamed; then he carried him up into the world, and showed him to Eurystheus, after which he brought him back to remain as the watch-dog of Hadês.

And so you see Heraclês led the life he had chosen when he was a young man; and these years of penance under Eurysthcus he spent in exploring thc world, and clearing it of dangerous monsters, and making it better for men to live in. I have not told you half his great deeds yet; many of thcm come in amongst his Labours, but it is convenient to keep the Twelve Labours together.

One of these deeds was the battle with the Giants. Zeus had already got rid of most of the ancient monsters, but a troop of giants remained, and to conquer these the oracle declared it necessary to seek the help of a mortal. Heraclês therefore was summoned to help; and the battle was joined on the plain of Phlegra.

The Giants, like other such, used huge rocks and trees to throw at their enemies, and burning fire-brands. One of them split off a chunk of the island Cos, and threw it at his enemy; you may see to-day how large it was, for it fell in the sea, and is now called the island of Nisyros. Another of them, Alkyoneus, whenever he was knocked down, jumped up again stronger than ever. For it was fated that he could not be killed upon the land where he was born. So the goddess Athena, who had plenty of sense, told Heraclês to drag him over the boundary of his land, into the next; and there they killed him easily enough.

Zeus struck some with his thunderbolt; Athena and Posei-
don, Apollo and Artemis, all took part, and Heraclês was
not wanting. The Giants were destroyed, and their bodies
were buried under volcanoes, and islands in the sea. So
now we see gods and men on the same side. Men were
becoming better, and Zeus was more friendly towards
them, for there was no more talk of destroying mankind.
And in fact, gods and men are now so mixed up that it
is impossible to tell of them separately.

Madness came upon Heraclês once more, which led
to a strange adventure. In his madness he killed a friend
without knowing what he did. When he recovered his
senses, he went to the oracle of Apollo, at Delphi, to ask
what he should do, in order to be made pure from this
deed of bloodshed; but the priestess would give him no
answer. This made him angry, and he said, "Very well, I
will make an oracle of my own!" Then he seized Apollo's
tripod, where the priestess used to sit, and began to carry
it off. As he went off, who should meet him at the door
of the temple but Apollo himself! Apollo took hold of
one leg of the tripod, Heraclês held to the other two, and
there was a great fight, Heraclês pulling one way and
Apollo the other. I do not know which would have won;
but while they were pulling away, Zeus came between
them. He said, "What is the meaning of this? No fighting
in the family, please; you will only break the thing, if you
pull it like that." Then he dropped a little speck of a
thunderbolt between them which fizzled up and startled
them both. "Now," he said, "put it back; and give Heraclês
his answer."

So Heraclês got his answer, and the answer was this:
he was to be sold as a slave, and to work for three years,
and then he was to pay the price paid for him to the soul
of the man he had killed.

So Hermês sold him, and he was bought by Omphalê,
Queen of Lydia, and she set him many tasks to do. Some
of them were worthy of Heraclês, for she made him clear
out the robbers and brigands from her country. One of
these was named the Stripper. He used to catch wayfarers,
and rob them, and make them dig about his vines with a
spade; Heraclês knocked him on the head with his own
spade.

There were also two brothers, full of mischief, who used to creep into the houses and steal. They must have been like a pair of ugly monkeys, for they were named Cerkôpês, which means Tailyboys. Their mother knew about their doings, but all she did was to give them a warning, "Ware Heraclês!"

Then one day Heraclês caught them. He trussed them up like a pair of fowls, and hung them head downwards on the two ends of a pole, and then he set off, carrying the pole across his shoulders, like a milkman. The boys were quite cheerful, and did nothing but crack jokes. "Who are you, pray?" they asked. He said, "I am Heraclês." As they were hanging head downwards, they had a good view of his legs, which were all covered with black hair; and one said, "You call yourself Hairyclês, do you? I call you Hairy-knees!" This pleased Heraclês, who liked a joke himself; so he let them off easily. Omphalê also liked a joke; so she used to make Heraclês put on her dress, and she put on his lion-skin, and then she gave him a distaff and spindle, and made him spin wool into thread. When the three years were up, he paid the fine, and he was now held to be free from guilt.

Heraclês also joined the quest of the Golden Fleece, a great adventure, but I leave that until I come to the story of the Argonauts. He also once met Theseus, a great hero like himself, and he had many other adventures which I must pass over; but there is one that I must tell, because that is the beginning of the story of Troy.

It begins in the early days of the reign of Zeus, when he had troubles without and troubles within. Only a hint has come down in memory; we only know that there was a conspiracy of the gods against Zeus. A party of them wanted to dethrone him, and put him in prison; and in this party was his wife Hera, and his daughter Athena, with his brother Poseidon, and his son Apollo. That might have been the end of Zeus, but for the sea-nymph Thetis, who was afterwards mother of Achillês. Thetis had a happy idea; why not call in the help of the hundred-handed monster, Briareos? And so he did: Briareos came to help his old friend, who had set him free once upon a time. You may imagine how it amazed the gods, plotting together in the corner, when they saw the monster march in, full of pride and power,

waving his hundred hands about, and saw him sit down by
the side of Zeus! Zeus punished Apollo and Poseidon, by
sending them down to earth, and commanding them to
serve the King of Troy for wages, one year long. They had
to build the walls of Troy, and hard work it was, as Poseidon
said afterwards; but when the year was up, and they asked
for their wages, the King gave them none; he only said,
"Get out, or I will cut off both your ears, and sell you to be
slaves in the islands!"

I suppose he did not know who they were, but he soon
found out, when they became gods again. For Apollo sent
a pestilence, and Poseidon sent a sea-monster, who caught
the people and swallowed them up. This went on until the
King enquired of an oracle, which told him that he would
be free if he gave his daughter to the monster. Accordingly
he left his daughter on the sea-shore, securely tied, for
the monster to eat. But he asked Heraclês to deliver her,
and promised that if he did, he would give as a reward his
precious mares to Heraclês: for he had some wonderful
mares of a divine breed. Then Heraclês attacked the mon-
ster. It was a terrible monster; Heraclês leapt into its
mouth, and went down into its belly; there he was three
days and nights, cutting and hacking, until he cut his way
out, and made an end of it at last.

So Heraclês killed the monster, and delivered the
maiden. He told her that she was free to go home, unless
she would rather come away with him; she said she
would rather come with him, for fear another monster
might come along later. But the King refused to give either
his daughter or the mares: he was as bad as ever, you see.
Then Heraclês went away, and soon came back with a
fleet; they besieged Troy, and broke through the wall, and
stormed the city. The King was killed, and Heraclês made
one of his sons King in his place. This man was called King
Priam, who comes in Homer's story of the great Trojan
War.

We are now coming to the last scene in the life of
Heraclês. His home now was in Calydon, a district in
North Greece, not far from the place where the English
poet Lord Byron died, in 1824, helping to make the Greeks
free. The King of Calydon had a beautiful daughter,
named Deïaneira, and she was wooed by the god of

the great river Acheloös, which runs through the country.
The wooer was rather alarming; for he appeared first in
the form of a bull, then in the form of a serpent with
shining coils, then like a man with a bull's head. You
may imagine that Deïaneira was pleased when a proper
man appeared, that is, Heraclês himself. There was a great
fight between Heraclês and the bull, but Heraclês won; and
the maiden became his wife. But she lived in great
anxiety, because Heraclês had to go away upon so many
adventures; and she was a little jealous too, for fear he
should fall in love with some one else, on his travels.

It happened that they had to travel away from Calydon
together; and on the way, there was a river to cross. At
the crossing, there was a Centaur, half man and half
horse, named Nessos, who used to ferry travellers over the
river. Heraclês told Nessos to carry over his wife; but when
Nessos was across on the bank, he laid hold of her, and
began to carry her off. Heraclês saw this from the other
side, and at once shot an arrow, which struck the death-blow
of Nessos.

But Nessos was an evil creature; and guessing that
Deïaneira might be jealous, he said to her, "Now I am
about to die, I wish to make up to you for my evil attempt.
Catch some of my blood as it drops from the wound, and
it shall be a charm for you; if your husband ever ceases
to love you, this charm will win back his love. Keep it
carefully away from the sun, and far from the fire, and
when you want to use it, put it like ointment upon him."
She caught the blood in a jar, and the Centaur died; and
she kept his blood secretly, with great care, sealed up in
the jar, away from fire and sunlight.

Now when Heraclês was coming back from one of his
adventures, victorious as usual, and with a long train of
captives, she found out that one of the captives was a very
beautiful maiden, and they said that Heraclês was in love
with her. So Deïaneira took out her jar, and poured the
blood upon the inside of a long robe which she had woven
herself, and sent it to her husband by a messenger. The
robe was folded up, and laid in a box to carry; she told
the messenger to give it to her husband, that he might wear
it when he did sacrifice in thanksgiving for a safe return.

But when the messenger was gone, she was terribly

frightened. As she was spreading the stuff upon the robe, a drop had fallen upon a piece of wool that lay near, and when the robe was gone, she happened to look at the wool, and saw that it was smouldering—then it broke into a flame, and all shrivelled up into ashes. She waited in great anxiety until the messenger should return; and there was good reason for it, for by and by the messenger did return, and she heard an awful story.

Heraclês took the robe, and put it on, and began his sacrifice. But the sunlight worked on the stuff through the robe, and he felt first a tickling, then a burning; the robe clung close to his limbs, and by degrees burnt into his flesh; they laid him down on a couch, and in a short time he perished. But his soul went to heaven, and there dwelt among the gods. They gave him a house to live in, and a heavenly bride, Hêbê, the goddess of youth; as if to say that Heraclês, after all his troubles, was to live for ever young and strong as he was in his youth. So the prophecy was fulfilled that he heard in his young days. He lived a noble life, he had many troubles, and in the end he gained fame and immortality.

XIV. *Typhon*

Zeus had his faults, but he was not a bad King; indeed, he was just the King who was wanted in those early days, when the chief need was to put things in order. Without order and discipline, you cannot have peace; and without power to punish, you cannot have order. Zeus had no courts of law, and no police, no army and navy; he had nothing but his own will and his own strength to back him. Anyone, with supreme power, is sure to make mistakes, however good he may be; and he is very likely to use his power sometimes to indulge his pleasures. Zeus did so, and so did the other gods.

Besides this, those who are kept in order do not always like it. The gods were an unruly company, and they were apt to rebel if they could, since each thought he could do the job better than Zeus, and wanted to be on the top. You have heard of one rebellion, and how it was put down, by the help of Briareos, who came in like a constable to keep order. I daresay there were other rebellions, but if so, they came to nothing.

Zeus had dangers from outside also to fight against. He had just conquered the Giants, as you have heard, but the last and worst of the monsters remained. Old Mother Earth, who had never forgiven Zeus for casting her sons into prison, made a last attempt to get the better of him. She produced her last offspring, last and most terrible, named Typhon, which we call in English the typhoon—that terrible water-spout which seems to join sea to clouds with a black tower, and rolls the waters round in a whirlpool, and bursts upon fleets of ships, so that they are never more seen.

The monster Typhon was more terrible still. From his shoulders grew a hundred dragons' heads, with black flickering tongues, and fierce fire blazed from their eyes. All manner of voices came out of the dragons' mouths. Sometimes they would utter words that the gods understood, for the gods had their own language; sometimes they would speak in the language of men; again it might be the noise of a bull bellowing in fury, or the roar of a ravening lion, or the hissing of serpents.

This monster was biding his time; and he found it through a fault of Zeus himself. For Zeus had fallen in love, and he left his post of duty; but as he did not wish to frighten the maiden, he hid thunderbolt and lightning in a rocky cave. But such things could not be hidden, for volumes of black smoke rolled from the cave, and sparks of fire shot out of the smoke, and the mountain rumbled. So Mother Earth saw it, and called to her son Typhon, "Up, Typhon, now is your time! I can show you where Zeus has hidden his lightning; take it, and fight him with his own weapons!"

Typhon came forth in his might. The dragons' heads, which were shaped like those of lions, tigers, bulls or horrid things without a name, stood out of his shoulders on monstrous necks, and every head roared or bellowed or hissed. Typhon seized the lightnings and the thunderbolts in his innumerable hands, and cast them over the skies.

Then indeed there was consternation in earth and heaven. The rocks melted, and the seas dried up; and all the constellations of the sky were shaken. You know perhaps that the stars of heaven, like everything else, had been coming into order. Here and there a number of them joined into groups, like families, and called themselves by various names; we call some of them the Signs of the Zodiac. These signs, twelve in number, are named in the following lines:

— names of animals!

> The Ram, the Bull, the Heavenly Twins,
> And next the Crab, the Lion shines,
>   The Virgin and the Scales,
>   The Scorpion, Archer, and the Goat,
>   The Man who bears the Watering-pot,
>   The Fish with shining tails.

There were many other groups; as the Great Bear, or Plough, or Charles's Wain, with its guardian, the Oxdriver; the Little Bear, the Swan, the Kids, the Snake, the Eagle, the Whale, the Great Dog, and the Little Dog and Orion the Hunter. Look up into the sky, and see how many of these you can make out. I am sure you know the Great Bear, but what about the others? Imagine now what a fuss there was among these! The Bull bellowed, the Lion roared, the Bear tried to climb up the North Pole, but Typhon pulled him down; he caught the Morning Star in one hand, and with another whipped up the horses of the Sun till they ran away; he threw the Bull across the sky, shining like a second Moon. The others did what they could: Orion shot at him, and his dogs barked, but the fixed stars alone stood immovable, far away from the fight.

Meanwhile, Zeus had returned from his excursion, and found his thunder and lightnings gone, and confusion all over the high heaven. What was he to do? He went down to earth, and there he met a man called Cadmos; you have not heard of Cadmos before, but I will tell you his story soon. So Zeus came to Cadmos, taking with him his friend Pan, and they gave him a flock of sheep and goats and a herd of cattle, and built him a hut of reeds. Pan gave him the panspipes, and Zeus said to him, "Pipe away, Cadmos, and we shall have peace in heaven. How old Cronos would laugh, if he could see me brought low by my own thunder-bolts! But I know these monsters. You can charm them with tootling, as you charm a serpent! And he is a hundred serpents!"

So Cadmos dressed up like a shepherd, and sat down

leaning against a tree, and tootled away on his pipes, where
Typhon could hear him. Typhon heard him, and pricked
up his ears, and crept towards the beautiful sound of the
pipes; but he left his lightnings behind him in the cave, deep
in the bosom of Mother Earth. He came up to Cadmos,
and held out one of his fifty right hands; he smiled as well
as he could with his middle face, a big one in the middle
of the hundred, which was in shape like a man's face, but
bright red in colour; and he opened his mouth, and said:

"Why do you fear me, herdsman? Why do you cover
your eyes with your hand? I will do you no harm; you may
keep your pipes and welcome, for I have another instru-
ment which has a voice of its own. Let us have a friendly
match. You make your reedy tune, and I will make a
thundery tune. Puff your cheeks and blow with your lips—
the blasts of the North Wind shall blow out my booming
thunderbolts! When I am King of Heaven, I will set you
there, cattle and all if you like, I will not part you from
them. You shall be close to the heavenly Goat, or if you
prefer it, beside the Bull. Pipe away, happy shepherd, to-
day on earth, to-morrow in heaven. You shall have Athena
to wife, or any other you like, except Hera; for I mean to
keep Hera for myself. If you have a brother who can drive
a team, he shall have the horses of the Sun. Pipe away, for
my victory! Your pipes shall be sounded in heaven, and
made equal to the heavenly harp!"

Cadmos made answer, "My pipes have pleased you a
little: what would you say if you could hear me play on
the harp? I had a harp once, but Zeus destroyed it, because
he was jealous for the sake of his son Apollo. But one of
these days we will have a match in heaven, Apollo and I.
When you strike down the others, be sure to spare him; and
then we will see which of us can sing best the praises of vic-
torious Typhon; and you must spare the Muses, that they
may dance for us."

Typhon nodded his heads in delight, and shook all his
locks of hair; and a shower of poison-drops was scattered
around. He thrust out all his heads, and pricked up all his
ears, and stood enchanted with the melody of the pipes.

While Typhon was listening to the tune, Zeus crept into
the cave, unseen and unheard, and once more took pos-
session of his lightnings and thunders.

What need is there to tell of the last battle? Typhon piled up rocks and crags for his two hundred hands to throw; and he shouted loud boasts to the winds. But when he has to face Zeus armed with his lightnings, Victory marching in front, with Fear on his right hand and Terror on his left, no monster can stand. Typhon was struck down, his eyes blinded, his hands all shrivelled up. The last revolt was ended; there were no more.

XV. *Cadmos*

Zeus, you remember, had come away from his post when the last monster appeared. He had seen a beautiful maiden in Phoenicia, where the Philistines were in the time of King David, but this was long before David's time. The maiden was Europa, and Zeus determined to carry her off. So he changed himself into a bull, and wandered along the shore. Europa was playing there with her friends: when she saw the bull, she was delighted with his looks, and ran up to pat his neck; she threw a wreath of flowers over his horns, and as he seemed to be friendly, she even climbed onto his back. Then the bull began to walk slowly about, and by degrees he came near to the sea. All at once, he set off running into the sea. Europa was very much frightened, but she did not dare to slip off; she held fast to his neck and back, clutching hold of the hairy coat; and very soon he was quietly swimming out to sea.

She cried loudly for help, and her friends all came running down to the beach. They stood in a row by the edge of the water, crying also, but that did no good; the bull swam on and on, and Europa cried till she was tired, then sank down on the bull's back, and made the best of it.

I have no doubt that Zeus could swim faster than most bulls; but even so, it was a long journey, until at last she espied land ahead. Zeus brought her to land in the island of Crete; and there he placed her in the sacred cave on Mount Dictê, where he had been kept as a baby. She lived long enough to bear two sons, named Minos and Rhadamanthys. We do not know much more about Europa, but she had the honour of giving her name to the continent of

Europe. Her son Minos became King of Crete, and Rhadamanthys became a famous judge. There is more to tell of them, but we must leave them now, and see what happened when she was carried off.

Her father was distressed at her loss, and sent off his sons to search for her, all over the world; but none of them ever found her. One of these sons was Cadmos, who met us in the last story. After many wanderings he came to Delphi and asked the oracle where he should find his sister.

Apollo gave him an oracle in these words:

> "Cadmos, you waste your time in wandering round
> To seek a bull that never can be found.
> Outside my sanctuary as you pass
> You'll see a dun cow feeding on the grass,
> Marked with a moon of white on either side;
> Follow her footsteps, let her be your guide;
> Follow her, till at length she lays her down;
> There in that place abide, and build a town."

Cadmos did as he was told. He followed the cow over hill and dale, until in the middle of a plain he came to a small hill with a spring flowing from it. There the cow lay down. But the spring was guarded by a terrible dragon, which darted forth and bit one man, and strangled another, until Cadmos's company ran off in dismay. But Cadmos caught up a huge stone, and heaved it at the monster. The stone crushed his head, and Cadmos ran in, and cut the head off with his sword.

It was a huge head, and the mouth was full of teeth. Cadmos pulled out all the teeth, and gathered them in a helmet; then he took out a handful of the teeth, and scattered them over the ground, like seed-corn. But as each tooth fell, up sprang from the place a warrior in full armour. Then this crop of warriors all began fighting with each other, until all were dead except five. Cadmos founded the city of Thebes; and the five survivors became the ancestors of the Thebans.

Cadmos did a great service to his new country, for he taught them the alphabet. Perhaps you will think there is not much in the alphabet; but suppose there were none, how would you write, and what would you read? Somebody must have invented the alphabet, and it was a very clever thing to do. I could tell you a long story about that which would surprise you; but there is no time now. You remember that Prometheus first taught men to write; but he made them draw pictures to begin with. If they wanted to write Tree, they drew a picture of a tree, and so on, and then he left them to learn more by themselves. They soon found it a long job to put everything into pictures. How would you write home in pictures, "Dear Father, please send me five shillings; your affectionate son, John"? Then some one hit on the idea of using the picture of a thing for the first letter of its name, as Tree for T, and so he could spell words which have no picture, like Time. Cadmos knew this plan, and he taught the alphabet to the Greeks; and thousands of years later, the Greeks taught it to the Romans; and the Romans passed it on to us. So when you write home for five shillings, remember Cadmos, who showed you how to do it. We still use one of his pictures at the beginning of the alphabet. For if you draw a cow's head and horns like

this ⊻ , you have only to turn it upside down, and then

you have a big A, which was the first letter of his word for a cow.

You have already heard how Cadmos helped Zeus, when the monster Typhone attacked him. For this help Zeus rewarded him by giving him a wife. This wife was Harmonia, herself of divine birth; for her father was Arês, god of war, and her mother was Aphroditê, goddess of love. Her name means friendship, and agreement, and anything that fits nicely together, like a tune of music, or a fine piece of carpentry; and we have borrowed her name in English for this kind of thing, when we use the word Harmony.

Cadmos and Harmonia had a grand wedding-feast; the gods were their guests, and sat upon golden thrones. This was the first time the gods ever attended the marriage feast of a mortal man. Many gifts were given, but the most famous was a necklace which one of the gods gave to Harmonia; it was a beautiful necklace, but afterwards it brought ruin on all who possessed it. Harmonia did not know that; but she found it out, and her four daughters found it out, when each of them perished in turn. Three of them I will leave for the present, but the fourth, Semelê, was the most famous of all.

For Zeus himself fell in love with Semelê, and made her his wife. But Semelê was not contented to be the wife of Zeus; she became jealous of Hera, the divine wife in Olympos, and forgot that she was only a mortal. Zeus did not forget; he never showed her his lightnings and his thunderbolts, as he did to Hera, and Semelê fretted and fumed and gave him no peace. Zeus warned her that it was dangerous, and told her she could not see him in all his glory and live; but you know he was rather too easy-going, and did not like to refuse what he was asked, so in the end he consented. He came to Semelê, with lightning and thunder playing about his head; and the lightning burnt her up. She perished therefore; but Zeus caught hold of her little baby, his own son, and took care of it as if he were the mother. The baby was the god Dionysos, or Bacchos, and I will tell you next what happened to him, and how he was admitted into the family of the Olympians. Zeus actually made a little pocket in his own leg, by cutting the skin, and there he kept the baby, like a kangaroo, until he could find a good nurse.

Zeus limp

XVI. *Dionysos* Son of Semelê

Hermês laughed when he saw Zeus limping about, with a pocket in his leg; and when Zeus opened the pocket, and pulled out the baby, and gave it to Hermês, and told him to find a nurse, Hermês said, "Let us name him Dionysos," or "Zeus's limp," for that is what the word meant, or so he said. Then he took the baby, and dandled him on his arm, and flew off to find a nurse. First he tried some nymphs; but Hera pursued the baby, and frightened the nymphs, and Hermês carried him off to his aunt, Ino, who *Aunt* nursed him with her own baby. Then she handed him over to a nursemaid, who took care of him all day, and kept on the watch for some trick of Hera's. She used to amuse him with a rattle and drums; she put a wreath of vine-leaves about his head, and wrapped up a pine-branch in ivy to play with. She dressed him in the dappled skins of fawns,

cool

and even wreathed a <u>festoon</u> of long snakes about his neck and arms.

what's that

But Hera pursued him still, wherever he went. Hermês, however, took care of him; and at last, after many adventures, he carried the baby to old Rheia, the Titan, mother of Zeus, who used to visit Asia Minor, and had her worshippers there. She used to ride in a car drawn by lions, and all round her were her attendants and guardians, the Corybants, who used to dance and clash their swords on their shields. Rheia taught the child to ride bareback on her lions, and to fear none of the wild beasts. When he was nine years old, he could catch hares by running on his own feet; he hunted the deer, and carried the tigers on his shoulders. He used to bring in lion-cubs as a gift for his grandmother, and even brought full-grown lions for her car. Zeus would laugh with joy to see it. When he grew older the boy used to dress in the skins of the wild beasts, and he had a car of his own, drawn by a team of leopards. He would put his hand into a bear's mouth, and the shaggy beast would lick the fingers, quite tame.

But now Dionysos was fully grown; and Zeus sent him a message by Hermês, in these words: "My boy, it is time you should earn a place in Olympos. You will not get it without hard work, for the gods have placed hard work in front of all good things. I did not win my own place without hard work, nor did my servant Hermês, who brings this message. He set Arês free from the brazen jar, and he killed the shepherd Argos, at my bidding. Perhaps you have not heard that story, so I will tell it to you.

"There was a beautiful maiden, Io, whom I loved dearly; but Hera was jealous, and turned her into a white cow. The cow was distracted, and ran after her father and sisters; she tried to say, I am Io, but all she could do was to give a gentle moo. They patted the pretty creature, and her father offered her a bunch of hay to eat; she only licked his hands, and dropped tears out of her eyes, but her tongue would not obey her wishes. Then she scratched in the sand with her hoof, first I and then O, over and over again. At last her father took notice, and understood that this was his daughter. But what could he do? He could only lament, and he could not even keep his daughter, for Hera soon sent her a guardian. This guardian was a won-

derful creature, named Argos, very strong, who had a circle
of eyes all round his head, and eyes spotted all over his
body: these eyes used to sleep in turn, a few at a time,
while the rest kept watch. Argos drove away her father,
and led Io into the mountains; he tethered her to a tree,
and sat down himself where he could watch the whole
country-side.

"But I called my servant Hermês, and told him to rescue
Io. Hermês put on his cap, and the wings on his feet,
and took his magic wand in his hand, and away he went
over hill and dale, until he came to the place where Argos
watched. When he came near the place, he laid aside his
cap and his wings, and gathered a flock of wild goats,
which was easy for a god to do; but he kept his magic wand
in his hand, and walked along like a goatherd, tootling upon
the pipes. Argos heard the tune, and called out, 'Come this
way, my friend, whoever you are. You might sit down with
me on this rocky seat; you will find here the best of food
for your goats, and it is a nice shady place for fellows like
us.' So Hermês sat down, and they passed the time in talk-
ing.

"Argos asked him, 'What is that pretty pipe of yours?'
'Oh,' he said, 'that is a long story. There was once a beauti-
ful nymph, and Pan fell in love with her.' Then he tootled a
tune, and went on, 'But the nymph did not like the looks of
Pan, with his horns and tail and goat's hooves, so she
ran away. She ran and ran till she could run no more: then
she came to a river, with reeds growing along the bank. She
plunged into the reed-bed, and cried to the reeds, "Save
me, my sisters!" And the reeds gathered all round her, and
she changed into the shape of the reeds herself. Then Pan
came running up, and saw her disappear into the reeds. He
clasped her in his arms, or what he thought was his nymph,
but found he was holding a bunch of reeds; and as he tried
to kiss her, and to whisper gentle words in her ear, the
breath of his lips made music among the reeds. "Ah well,"
he said, "I will keep you always with me"; and he arranged
a row of reeds on a frame, and carried them with him
wherever he went; whenever he wanted to kiss the nymph,
or to whisper to her, he blew upon the reeds, and made this
lovely tune which you hear. And the pipes bear the name

of Syrinx, which was the name of the nymph, and the reeds are called Syrinx too.'

"But before he finished his tale, what with the tale and what with the talking, Argos became sleepy, and his eyes began to close. Now Hermês took his magic wand, which with a touch can send waking eyes to sleep, and stroked round the head of Argos, and stroked down his body, until all his eyes were fast closed in sleep, and his head nodded down on his breast: then Hermês took up his sickle, and with one blow cut off Argos's head.

"I will not tell you now what happened to Io, because that is another long story; for Hera sent a gadfly to sting her, and drove her wandering all over the world, where she had many adventures, until at last she was happy. But Hera took all the eyes of her servant Argos, and set them in the peacock's tail, where they are to this day, and that is why the peacock is her favourite bird. But I leave all this, for it is Hermês I wish to tell of now, and how he won a place among the Olympians. Just as he won his place by good service, so must you. Like Io, you must travel all over the world, and you must do what you can for mankind."

You remember that Dionysos had been taught by Rheia how to tame the wild beasts; and in the stories about him, he is often represented as a bull, a bear, or lion, or panther. He had also learnt from her the secrets of her worship, and how to play on the flute and the timbrel and the drum. And he made a wonderful discovery, the fruit of the vine.

For he had a beloved friend and playmate, who died, and Dionysos would not be comforted. But his friend was buried, and from the place where he lay buried grew up a plant, with leaves curling like the boy's hair, and clusters of grapes blushing like the boy's cheeks. Dionysos caught a cluster of grapes, and squeezed it in his hand, and the juice trickled into a hollow horn which he had in the other hand. He touched the horn with his lips, and tasted the juice, and as he drank, his sorrow went from him. He cried out:

"There is life in you still, my friend! Figs and olives are good, and so is wheaten bread, but they give pleasure only as far as the tooth. You run through all my veins like my blood, and my friend becomes a part of me! Here is my nectar, and Olympos can have no better. You shall give joy to the feast; when men shall drink of you, those who are poor will become rich, those who mourn will forget their sorrow."

After this, wherever he went he was attended by troops of followers: old Seilenos, a lover of wine, but sage and prudent; frisky Satyrs, bold as lions before a fight, timid as hares in the fight; women maddened with wine, for they never knew when to stop; nymphs, and graces, and dancing maids. They dressed in the skins of fawn or panther, and put on their heads wreaths of vine or ivy, and twined serpents about their arms and necks. Each held a long fennel-stalk, or a light rod, with ivy twined round it and a fir-cone on the top. All night long they used to dance, waving torches of pine-wood, to the music of drums and flutes. Dionysos led his troops all over the world, even as far as India, and sometimes he had to fight battles; but in the end, he gave to all mankind his precious gift of wine. But he was careful to warn them not to drink too much. If they were moderate, they had nothing but joy; but if they took more and more, they became angry and quarrelsome, and violent, and did evil deeds. He showed them how to mix water with their wine, that they might not be maddened by it.

Dionysos had many adventures. Once he was standing upon a rocky headland, looking like a young man, with long hair flowing over his shoulders, and clad in a purple robe. A ship passed by; and the mariners saw him there, and made a plot to carry him off, and make some profit by him. So they ran ashore, and surrounded him, and carried him on board ship. They tied him fast with ropes; but the ropes slipped off his limbs, and left him free. The steersman called out, "You fools, do not you see this is a god? Zeus perhaps, or Apollo, or Poseidon? You cannot hold him: let us put him back on shore." But the captain said, "You lend a hand with the sail, and then look to the wind. You may be an old woman, but there are men here to look after that fellow. He will soon send word to his family, and there will be a good ransom, now that we have got him by a piece of good luck."

So they hoisted the sail, and got under way: and then miracles began to happen. Wine ran down the mast, and a

beautiful scent was spread abroad. Vine-leaves and tendrils
budded out of the sails on each side, and bunches of grapes
hung down, while ivy crawled up the mast. Suddenly a lion
appeared on the forecastle, and roamed about, and amid-
ships a shaggy bear, growling and glaring. All the crew
huddled together upon the poop. The lion leapt on the
captain, and tore him to pieces; the other seamen dived
into the sea, and as they dived they were turned into dol-
phins. But Cionysos spared the worthy steersman, and
made him a happy man.

Old Seilenos himself had an adventure which is worth
telling. He was fond of wine as you have heard, and once
he took too much wine and went to sleep. While he was
asleep the country people found him, and tied his hands
together, and led him to their King, Midas, King of Phrygia
in Asia Minor. "See here," they said, "my lord King, what
a queer creature we have found! He seems to be only half
a man—look at his tail!"

But Midas knew the old man; so he said, "Let him go.
I know him; he is a friend of Dionysos." The countrymen
untied his hands, and Midas took him back to Dionysos
himself.

"Oh, here is my friend!" said Dionysos. "I thought you
were lost for good! And you, my worthy Midas, you de-
serve a reward: ask what you will, you shall have it."

Midas was a rich man, but like many rich men, he wanted
to be richer; so he said at once, "I ask that everything I
touch may turn into gold!"

Dionysos could not help thinking this was a greedy wish;
but he had promised, and he said, "Be it so: everything you
touch shall turn into gold."

Midas went off delighted. He plucked a twig from a
tree—twig, leaves, and all turned into gold. He touched a
stone—the stone turned into gold. He patted his favourite
dog—the dog at once froze into gold, and stood there, a
golden image! Midas did not know whether to be glad or
sorry at that, but he kept his fingers from his attendants,
for fear they might turn into gold too.

When he came home, he had recovered his spirits a little,
and he said, "Let us have a grand feast to-night, to cele-
brate this occasion." He was careful to eat nothing mean-

while, so that he might have more room for the feast when it came.

The feast was ready, the courtiers were in their places, and Midas began by taking up a goblet of wine, to drink their health. "Your good health, gentlemen!" he cried, and raised it to his lips. The goblet was gold already; but as soon as the wine touched his lips, it turned into liquid gold. He did not like this at all, and spat out the drop he had taken. "What's this!" he cried, but nobody else knew what it was; they only looked at him in surprise. He sat down, and took up a piece of bread—it turned into gold. He passed a bit of game to his lips—it turned into gold. The guests were eating and drinking away comfortably, and did not notice the King, until he suddenly said, "Look here, all my food is turning into gold, and I shall starve!"

How they all stared at him, and tried not to laugh. They gave him titbits with their own hands, but no sooner did the food touch his lips, than it was gold. The King left the table, and went to his room, and spent a very unhappy night.

Next day things were no better, and he went off posthaste to Dionysos. When he found the god, Midas looked so pale and unhappy, that Dionysos asked, "Why, what is the matter?"

Midas said, "Your gift!"

Dionysos said, "What is the matter with my gift? Didn't it come off?"

"Only too well!" said Midas. "All my food turns to gold, and I shall just starve to death!"

"Well," said Dionysos, "I gave you what you asked, so don't blame me. However, if you are tired of it, go down to the river Tmolos, and bathe in the water."

Off went Midas, as fast as he could, and bathed in the river Tmolos, and all the gold was washed out of him into the river. And ever afterwards, you had only to sift the sands of the river, and specks of gold were found there, as they still are, I believe.

Midas was a stupid old man, as you see, and now he was so sick of gold, that he spent his time in wandering about the woods. One day he found a contest going on between Apollo and Pan. Old Pan was proud of his pipes, and chal-

lenged Apollo to a musical match; so they met in a glade of
the woods, and chose a judge, and Pan piped away, and
Apollo played on the harp. Meanwhile Midas had crept
up, and hid in a bush, all ears. He was delighted with the
music, but on the whole he preferred Pan.

When the judge was asked, "Which is the better?" he
said at once, "Apollo"; but Midas could not contain him-
self, and he sang out from his bush, "I think Pan is the
best myself!"

"Who is that?" cried Apollo, and pulled him out from
the bush. "Why, it is King Midas, the man of gold!" and
he laughed aloud. "So you think Pan is better than I am,
do you?"

"Yes, I do," said Midas.

"Well," said Apollo, "you have not much of an ear. I
will give you a better pair." Then he waved his hands, and
Midas's ears grew up about a foot high, and covered them-
selves with fur and fluff, and lo and behold, Midas had a
fine pair of ass's ears. "There you are," said Apollo; and as
Midas listened to him, he did not turn his head towards
him, as a man does, but waggled his two ears in that direc-
tion, like an ass, and all the company roared with laughter.

Midas went off in a great state, and slunk indoors after
dark. He went up to his chamber, and told his slave to wrap
a grand turban about his head, to cover the ears. "Now
then, young man," he said, "not a word to anyone, or off
comes your head." Then he went into his court, and nobody
was the wiser.

But the wretched slave did not know what to do. He was
amazed and dumbfounded, and bursting with a fine piece
of gossip which he durst not tell to a soul. Imagine how you
would feel with such a piece of news, if your master had a
long pair of ass's ears, and you could not tell anyone! He
kept it to himself as long as he could; and when he could
hold it no longer, he rushed down to the river-side, and dug
a deep hole, and whispered into the hole, "Midas has a
pair of ears like a jackass!" Then he filled up the hole with
earth, and came home again, feeling much better.

But that was not the end of it. Reeds grew up out of
the hole, and there was a great rustling among the reeds,
and some boys who were surprised at the noise happened
to listen, and this is what they heard, a loud whisper carried

through the air—"Midas has the ears of a jackass! Midas has the ears of a jackass!" They told their friends, and before long everybody about the court was whispering, and choking with laughter, "Midas has the ears of a jackass under that fine turban!"

At last Midas himself caught the whisper, and the courtiers could see his whole turban waggle as his ears turned to the sound. He was furious, and I am afraid the slave's head was cut off, but now the King had to make the best of it.

Dionysos carried his wine all over Greece, and found worshippers everywhere, who built him temples; and everywhere those who used his gift well were made happy by it, and those who used it badly were made furious or mad. So it is with all the gifts of God. They are given to us for use, not for misuse, and we learn by experience.

Lastly, having done his work in the world, Dionysos wished to take his place in Olympos; but he would not go without his mother, Semelê. She was a mortal, and she had died, and now she was in the dark house of Hadês; so Dionysos resolved to go and fetch her. But he did not know the way, until a man who knew told him. There was a pool in the marsh of Lerna, where Heraclês had his fight with the water-snake, if you have not forgotten; this pool was bottomless, and that was one way to the lower world.

Dionysos dived in, and in due time came to the dark house of Hadês. He begged for his mother's life; and King Hadês, who was never willing to let anyone go when once he had them, refused at first; but at last he agreed, if Dionysos would send him down in exchange one of those whom he loved best, a life for a life. Dionysos promised, and led his mother up once more to the earth, where she had been so happy and so unhappy, and thence to Olympos, where they both joined the company of the immortal gods. He did not forget his promise to Hadês. What he loved most on earth were three things, the vine, the ivy, and the myrtle; so he sent Hadês a myrtle plant, a life for a life. Perhaps that was not quite a fair exchange; what do you think?

You may still see the place where Dionysos dived, on his way to the house of Hadês. It is a pool of dark waters, smooth and glassy, with great reeds growing round it, and a circle of tall white poplars with silvery stems. The people still say that it is bottomless. You may still see the place where he came up with his mother, a beautiful plain on the bay of Troizen, with groves of oranges and lemons, and rows of tall cypress trees. But the deep cleft in the rock by which they came is closed now for ever.

XVII. *Asclepios*

One more god has to be added, and then the number of the Olympians will be complete. After that we have to do with their dealings among mankind. This god was named Asclepios, and he was the god of healing, one who did only kind things, and never pushed out anyone else; but all men loved him and worshipped him for his deeds of kindness.

He was the son of Apollo; but when he was born, he was left out among the mountains, to live or die. There a nanny-goat found him, and gave him milk, and a dog watched over him, until a shepherd came and found him. He was in charge of a wonderful creature named Cheiron, a Centaur; that is to say, he was half man and half horse.

Cheiron was himself the son of old Cronos the Titan; and he lived in a cave on Mount Pelion. He was the wisest and most just of all creatures on earth. He knew all the healing herbs that grow, to cure the diseases which men have; he could heal wounds, and sing magical ditties which soothed the sick and made them well. He could chase and catch the wild animals. In his cave among the hills he lived a happy life at home with his wife and mother; and all the young heroes used to be brought to him, and left to be taught, like schoolboys in a boarding school. He taught them how to ride on his own back, and how to hunt, and how to fight, and how to use healing herbs; and he taught them the rules of good conduct. His most famous rule was, Honour Zeus first among gods, and among men honour first thy father.

Asclepios learnt all this from him, but he paid most attention to the healing herbs, and the salves for curing wounds, and the magical ditties; for he cared nothing about hunting or war. When he grew up, he became famous for his cures; but he went too far in this. He happened one day to kill a snake; and as the dead snake lay on the ground, by and by another snake crept up, and laid a herb on the dead snake's mouth. Then the dead snake came to life again, and they both went away together. Asclepios noticed what the herb was—for he had not learnt about this one from Cheiron; and he used it to bring a dead man back to life.

This made Hadês angry, and he complained to Zeus. "Look here, sir," he said, "if this man goes on, my kingdom will be empty. It is not fair to me." Then Zeus struck Asclepios with a thunderbolt, and killed him. But Apollo his father begged Zeus to relent, and Zeus revived Asclepios, and placed him among the stars. I do not think he used to visit Olympos, and to join the company of the gods there. He seems to have been much more interested in mankind, and did not care for grandeur. He soon had temples all over Greece, and men were glad to worship him.

These places were much more than temples. Besides the temple, there was always a place where sick people could stay, while they were being cured. They used to lie in rows along a sort of portico, like what you see outside a house, only much longer, and much finer, built of stone, with pillars, and open on the warm side. There in the night they had dreams, and the dreams told them what to do to be cured. Or else the god himself, with his sons and daughters, used to make the rounds, and give the sick people medicines or ointments.

He had several sons and daughters, who helped him. Three of the daughters were named Health, and Healing, and Allcure, and we have actually borrowed two of their names in English. One of them is "Panacea," which we use to mean a drug that cures everything; and one is Hygieia, which people who like long words use instead of health when they talk about "hygiene," just to show off. Besides the sons and daughters, the god used to be helped by his famous snakes. These snakes lived in a hole under the temple, and they used to crawl about among the sick people, and lick their eyes or their wounds. In the morning, the proper thing was to drop a cake into the snakes' hole, besides making a sacrifice to the god.

You may still see the ruins of some of these places, and the thank-offerings of those who were healed. Sometimes they used to give a little model of what was cured: an eye, if they had sore eyes, or a tooth, or an arm or leg. Sometimes they put up the story of what happened, carved on the stones of the wall. One of them says he had had a lance-head in his jaw for six years. He slept in the corridor; and dreamt the god came, and drew it out, and put it into his hands. Next morning, he woke, and found the lance-head in his hand. Another man had a long beard and a bald head, and the boys used to laugh at him, which he did not like; but the god put some ointment upon his head, and in the morning he found a fine crop of hair.

When the Greek gods came to an end, and the Christian religion took their place, the Christian churches took over some of their ancient customs. So even now, sick people come, and sleep in the courtyard of a church; and if they are healed, they offer to the saint of the church little silver models of hands, or feet, or teeth, or the whole body, whatever part may have been ailing. Thus we may think that the kind, good Asclepios is not quite dead and finished, even now.

PART 3

XVIII. *Jason*

We now come to one of the most wonderful stories, the Quest of the Golden Fleece; and I must tell you how it began.

Jason was the son of a man who was rightful king of a place in Thessaly: but the king's cousin, Pelias, took the kingdom for himself. The banished king could do nothing. A son was born to him, and he was afraid that Pelias might kill the child; so he pretended that the child was dead. The women set up a loud lamentation in the house, they beat their breasts, they tore their hair, as the fashion was; finally, they made a funeral, and draped the bier with purple, and pretended to bury the child. But what they really did was this: they put the child in charge of faithful persons, and sent him away secretly, by night, into the mountains, to the cave of the Centaur Cheiron. You remember Cheiron the Centaur, half man and half horse, who was the son of Cronos the old Titan; he had been trained in hunting and gymnastics—as far as a horse could manage—in music and medicine, and in the art of prophecy. He knew all about all the animals on the hills, and all the trees of the forest, and all the herbs of healing which grow in the ground. Indeed, he became the wisest of creatures, kind and good. He lived in a cave on Mount Pelion, with his wife and his old mother, and it was the custom to send young boys to him, like a sort of training school for the heroes. He taught all his boys to honour Zeus, and to honour their fathers, besides the arts I have mentioned. So to him Jason came; and there he remained for twenty years, learning to be a brave man, and a wise man.

Now Pelias was always uneasy in his mind. He knew

he had no right to be king, and he feared the gods might punish him; so he became more anxious than ever, when a strange oracle was given him by Apollo, "Beware of the man with one understanding!" He could not quite make out what this meant, and he brooded over it, as he was meant to do.

Then one day he heard everybody in the palace talking about a piece of news. "Have you heard?" they said. "A young fellow has just appeared in the market-place, a stranger. He is dressed in a close-fitting tunic, with a leopard skin thrown over it; he carries a pair of spears, and he has thick chestnut hair falling to his shoulders. Come and see!"

They came to see, but no one knew him. "A fine fellow, this!" they said. "He can hardly be Apollo, or the god of war, and those big boys, Otos and Ephialtês are dead, as we know. But who can he be?"

Pelias came to see also. He got into his mule-car, and came galloping along the street. When he saw the man, he was struck with fear; for he had one foot bare, and a boot on his right foot only, since he had lost the other in crossing a river. When Pelias saw this, he thought, "Here is the man with one understanding!" That is quite a good name for a boot, isn't it? No doubt Apollo meant to puzzle Pelias. And Pelias was very much afraid; but he hid his fear, and to hide it, he spoke very rudely to the young man. "Where do you come from, young stranger?" he said. "What old drab was your mother, what ditch were you born in? Tell the truth, and do not try to deceive me."

But Jason returned a soft answer. "Sir, I will show you what Cheiron's training is; for I come from his cave, and from the gentle breeding of his mother and his wife. Twenty years I have spent there, and I have never done a deed or said a word to make them ashamed of me. Now I come to my own home and claim the honour which is mine by inheritance. For I am informed that Pelias has robbed my father of his rights. And now can any of you kind people tell me where my father lives? I am Jason, the son of Aison."

They led him to the place, and his father knew him, and wept for joy to see his beautiful son. Soon his two brothers came from their homes, and his cousins, and there was a family feast. Jason did the honours; and after they had feasted and talked, he said, "Now for a serious word. Come with me to Pelias, and let us hear what he will say."

Straight from the feast they made their way to the palace; and there Jason said, still speaking gently:

"My lord, I do not complain or threaten. We ought to rule our passions, and so to act that happiness may follow. You and I are of the same race, and it is a shame for kinsmen to quarrel and fight. Keep your flocks and herds, keep your house and your wealth; but give me the sceptre and the throne which belonged to my father, that no violence may arise between us."

Pelias answered, "I will do as you wish. I am old, and you are young, and you may be able to quell the anger of the gods below. For Phrixos bids me bring him home, and the golden fleece of the ram which saved him. That is what he tells me in a dream; I have enquired of Apollo's oracle, and he tells me the same. Go to the far east, and bring them back, and I swear an oath to you that I will hand over my throne to you." So they agreed; but before I tell you how Jason accomplished the quest, I must tell the story of the ram with a golden fleece.

XIX. *The Ram with a Golden Fleece*

Phrixos was the son of the King of Boeotia, and he had a sister named Hellê; their mother was Nephelê, the Cloud. It must be awkward to have a Cloud for your wife; you never know when she will be at home, and when she will be flying about in the sky. And so the King seems to have found it; for he married a second wife, named Ino, who was óne of the daughters of Cadmos. You remember Cadmos, no doubt, and his wedding, and the necklace given to his wife, which brought misfortune wherever it went. It brought misfortunes to Ino, one of them a very great misfortune, that is, jealousy, which makes the person who has it miserable, and every one who comes near miserable too. Ino had children of her own, and she was jealous of Phrixos and Hellê, and wanted to get rid of them.

So she made the following plan. First, she got hold of

the seed-corn which was to be sown in the land for next year; and she had it all parched, over the fire, so that it was dead, and could not grow. Then she put it back where it came from. In due time, the corn was sown; but no shoots came up—there was not a leaf, or an ear of corn, in the whole country. The people were in despair and did not know what to do.

Next, Ino persuaded her husband to enquire of the oracle at Delphi; and when he sent to enquire, she bribed the messengers who went there. She told them then to come back and pretend that they had asked the oracle, and that the oracle said, "Kill Phrixos and Hellê at the altar for a sacrifice, or your corn will grow no more." This was a dreadful blow to the King; but he had to obey what he believed to be God's wish, like Abraham and Isaac in the Bible. And in this case too there was a ram, but a different sort of ram from the ram which was sacrificed instead of Isaac.

This was a wonderful ram, with a golden fleece, which Nephelê from the clouds provided at the altar. There stood the two children, ready to be killed; there stood the sacrificer with his knife; there stood the King, full of sorrow, and jealous Ino, full of joy; and lo and behold, down came the golden ram, and up got the boy and girl upon his back, and away he flew into the sky.

For a long time, all was well; they passed over land and sea, making for the far east. But after a while, Hellê grew tired, and could not hold on any longer. She just dropped down into the sea, and was drowned; and the place where she fell is still called Hellespont, or the Sea of Hellê.

Phrixos could do nothing, and the ram went on, until he came to the far end of the Black Sea, to the east, to the land of the Colchians; and there he came down. The King of this land was named Aiêtês, the brother of the witch Circê, whom you will hear of in the story of Odysseus, if you can find some one to tell it to you. The ram was sacrificed, and his golden fleece was nailed to a tree in a sacred grove of oaks, and guarded by a terrible dragon which never slept.

This Phrixos, who was a cousin of Pelias and of Jason, was the man who appeared in a dream to Pelias, and told him to bring him back home, and lay his ghost. At least, that was what Pelias said; but perhaps he made it up, because he thought that Jason would probably be killed in trying to get the Golden Fleece.

King Aiêtês gave his daughter to Phrixos, when he was old enough to marry, and there he lived and died. But his sons returned to their father's old home, to claim his inheritance. And ever after they had to obey a strange rule. The eldest son, the head of the family, was never allowed to enter the town-hall. He might go anywhere else he liked, but if he entered the town-hall, he could not got out again unless he were taken to the altar, and sacrificed on the spot. You will not be surprised to hear that the eldest sons, from generation to generation, preferred to go away and settle in some foreign land.

XX. *The Argonauts*

You know now what a task Jason had to do. People knew very little about the world, then; and they had only very small sailing ships, or galleys that used oars, in which they were at the mercy of winds and waters. This voyage was aimed at the far end of the Black Sea, a dangerous sea which no one knew well: indeed, its proper name was the Unfriendly Sea; only men called it the Friendly Sea for fear of offending it. A noble ship was built for the voyage; the goddess Athena helped in the building, and set up as the stem a great beam of oak, which was brought from the sacred grove at Dodona. This great oaken stem had a voice, and spoke sometimes to the crew. The ship was named Argo, and the sailors were called the Argonauts, or Sailors of Argo.

All the great heroes of Greece came to take part in the voyage: their names you will hear often in Greek story. Heraclês came, with Castor and Polydeucês, all sons of Zeus; Orpheus came, the great singer; Holdfast and Pullhard, sons of Hermês; Zetas and Calaïs, sons of the North Wind, and each had a pair of wings on his shoulders, shivering with purple feathers; Tiphys the steersman, and Mopsos the seer. And there on the shore was the old Centaur Cheiron, with his wife, who held young Achillês on

her arm, to wish good-bye to his father Peleus, and a happy
voyage.

Across the Aegean Sea they sailed, and through the
Hellespont, where Hellê had fallen and died; and over the
Propontis, a little sea between Hellespont and Bosporos,
where they had many adventures. They had to fight with a
tribe of huge men, who had six arms; two grew from their
shoulders, and four from their sides. In one place, where
they went to get water, they lost the boy, Hylas. As he let
down his urn into a pool, the nymph of the pool saw this
beautiful boy, and stretched up her arm to embrace him; she
loved him so much, that she drew him down to the water,
and he was seen no more. But Heraclês sought for him high
and low, and he wandered so far, that the others put off
without missing him, and left him behind. When they found
he was missing, they were about to turn back for him; but
a sea-god put up his head and shoulders out of the water,
and said, "Why do you wish to take Heraclês in search of the
Golden Fleece? It is his duty to serve King Eurystheus, and
to perform the labours which the King ordains." So they
went on, and Heraclês went about his proper work.

Again they had to put in, to the place where poor old
Phineus lived by the sea. He had the gift of foretelling the
future, and he told too much; so blindness was sent upon
him by Zeus, and he was persecuted by the Harpies. These
were huge great birds, with sharp wings and claws. When-
ever Phineus took a meal, the Harpies would swoop down
upon him from the clouds, and snatch the food from his
hands, and even from his mouth: worse than that, they cov-
ered the rest of it with filth, so that he could not eat any of
it, and he had to live by what kind neighbours brought him
secretly. This was to cease, as he knew by his power, when
Jason should come and deliver him.

He heard the tramp of the heroes, and came down to
meet them, like a lifeless dream, bowed over his staff, and
crept to the door on his withered feet, feeling the walls; his
limbs trembled for weakness, and his parched skin was
caked with dirt, and only the skin held his bones together.
He sat on the threshold of the courtyard, and the earth
seemed to reel under his feet. At last he said:

"Listen, brave men, if you are they whom Jason leads
in the ship Argo. Save me, and leave me not in my misery.

I am blind, as you see, and I can eat no meat; for the Harpies snatch the food from my mouth, and bespatter all the place with filth. The oracle declares that I shall be saved by the sons of the North Wind, and let me tell you, I am no stranger to them, for their sister was my wife."

So they got ready a feast, the last prey for the Harpies. And no sooner had he touched the food, than out of the clouds swooped the horrible birds, like flashes of lightning, and clutched the food from the old man's hand, and sped away over the sea. But the two sons of the North Wind unfolded their purple wings, and sped away in pursuit, holding their swords in hand. They came up with the Harpies, until they just grazed their feathers with their finger-tips; and they would have destroyed them, but Iris, the messenger of the gods, met them, and said, "It is not lawful to kill the hounds of Zeus, but I swear to you that they shall visit old Phineus no more." So they turned back, and the Harpies flew on to their den in distant Crete.

The heroes washed the old man's skin, and made sacrifices, and set out a new feast, which he enjoyed, for the first time in many long years. And the old man said, "Listen now, and I will tell you what it is lawful for you to know. For I have learnt that Zeus desires to reveal his oracles to men incomplete, that they may not know too much. But this I may tell you. You will soon see, at the mouth of the Bosporos, two rocks, called the Clashers, which constantly clash together, and then move apart. You must take with you a dove, and when you come to the rocks, let her go; then watch if she passes through. If she escapes, you may follow; and row hard, for in that passage, rowing will be better than praying. But if she is caught, then turn back; for it is better to yield to God's will." Then he told them of other perils, and said that they should reach their goal, and that a god would guide them on their way home. Lastly he said, "Take thought of Aphroditê, goddess of love, for your success will depend upon her help. I may tell you no more."

Then the two sons of the North Wind returned, panting from their long chase, and said, "Sir, you are free from the Harpies for ever."

When the time came for departure, the heroes embarked, not forgetting to take the dove with them.

At the mouth of the Bosporos, they saw two huge rocks rushing violently together: the rocks met with a crash, and sent up the sea in clouds of spray; then they leapt apart, and the sea rushed in to fill the gap, and met in the middle, rising like a great mountain of water. There was a swift current against them, and a wind blowing them on, which nearly matched, so they were obliged to put out the oars.

As the rocks drew together again, they let the dove go, and all craned their necks to see. Clash! went the rocks; as they went back, the heroes could see the dove had got through, only the rocks had caught one of her tail-feathers. They were able to see this, because one of them, named Lynceus, had eyes so sharp, that he could see everything under the sky, as clearly as if it were close.

The waves whirled the ship round; but the helmsman shouted out—"Row, you men! She's through!" and they rowed with all their might. As the rocks moved apart, a huge wave rose up in front of them, and carried them back; but another wave rose behind them and carried them onwards. The rocks were now rushing together again, nearer and nearer, but the men rowed as they never had rowed before, and the wave carried them out clear into the sea. The two rocks crashed together, and there they remained, joined into one: they stood still, and they have never moved since.

Then the heroes gave thanks to Athena, who had built the ship Argo so strongly that she was proof against all the perils of the sea.

They passed on, and came in due time to the island of Arês, where old Phineus had told them to land. This island was haunted by flocks of terrible birds, with brazen beaks and brazen feathers; you remember these, how Heraclês had scared them away from the Stymphalian lake. These birds used to shoot out their feathers like arrows; and the first notice of them which the heroes had, was that one of them shot out a bronze feather, and it struck one of the heroes on his shoulder.

"What's that?" he cried in dismay. Some one drew out the feather, and bound up the wound; and another said, "These are the birds of Arês! It is of no use to shoot arrows against them, they are too many and too strong; but I remember what Heraclês did, for I was there and saw it. He shook a rattle of brass, and frightened them away. Let us divide ourselves; one half shall row, and one half shall put on their helmets, with nodding plumes, and hold up their spears, and make a roof over the rowers with their shields. When we come near the island, these will shout, and rattle the spears on the shields."

So they did. They shouted and rattled, and the birds shot their feathers in clouds, but they crashed on the shields and only made a louder din. So the birds were frightened, and all flew away to the mountains opposite.

The heroes landed, and now they found out why Phineus had told them to land there; for on the shore they found the four sons of Phrixos himself, who had set out for home in order to claim their inheritance, and here they had been shipwrecked. They were glad to get on board, and Jason hoped they might be useful when the ship came to Colchis.

The heroes sailed away, and coasted along by the Caucasos Mountains, where Prometheus was nailed to a rock. There they saw the great eagle, sailing high, near the clouds, and they heard the whirr of his wings, and the fanning of the wings shook their sails, high as he was. He sailed along with his wings pushed far out on both sides, like a ship with long shining oars. And soon they heard the bitter cry of Prometheus, as the eagle swooped down and tore at his liver. At last they came to the Colchian land; they entered the mouth of the river, and let the ship ride at anchor off the shore.

XXI. *Cupid and His Mother*

While the heroes were hidden among the reeds, their friends in Olympos were not forgetful of them. Hera in particular sought out Athena, and said, "What shall we do about the Golden Fleece? Do you think Jason will be able to persuade King Aiêtês to part with it? He has a wonderful tongue to persuade, and he always loves gentle words. Or will they have to fight for it? And how can so few fight against so many? Give me your advice."

Athena said, "Really I do not know what to say. I have

been considering many plans, but I cannot think of a good one."

They were silent awhile, with their eyes fixed on the ground. Then Hera said:

"I will tell you what. The king's daughter, Medeia, is skilled in all sorts of charms and spells. Would she help? What if she were to fall in love with Jason? Suppose we ask the help of Aphroditê."

"Well," said Athena, "I do not understand those things, I never cared much myself for gods or men, but by all means let us try."

So they went to the house which Hephaistos, the smith-god, had built for Aphroditê when he married her. He was away at the forge; but they found the goddess on a seat facing the door. Her golden hair was loose, and covered her shoulders; she was parting it with a golden comb, and just about to bind it up into braids. When she saw them, she rose, and greeted them, and gave them seats, gathering up her long hair in one hand, and said:

"Good friends, what brings you here? I have not seen you this long time; you do not often visit my humble home."

She said this, because her husband was not quite of the first rank, and Hera disliked him, although he was her own son. Aphroditê thus felt her vanity hurt a little. But Hera said:

"Ah, you are making fun of us! But this is a serious matter which we come about. Jason and his company are now on the river Phasis, in quest of the Golden Fleece, and I do not see how they can get it. Jason at least I am determined to save. I cannot abide that Pelias, who neglects my sacrifices; but I do love the young man. Once I was on earth, trying men, to see how they behaved: I took on me the likeness of an ugly old crone, and sat down by the side of a rushing river, when he came along. Then I begged him to help an old woman, and he took me up on his shoulders, ugly though I was, and carried me across the river. So I will certainly save him, and punish Pelias for his neglect."

"Well," said Aphroditê, "what can I do? I will help you if I can."

Hera said, "You can help us, indeed. Just tell your boy

Cupid to shoot one of his arrows at Medeia, and make her
fall in love with Jason."

"Ah, if he will!" said Aphroditê. "He is a naughty boy,
and will not do what I tell him. He is more likely to listen
to you than to me. I mean to break his bow and arrows
before his eyes, the little wretch! And he says that if I
touch him, he will make me repent it!"

The goddesses smiled, and looked at each other. This
vexed Aphroditê, and she went on, "Yes, you only laugh
at my troubles; I get no sympathy from any one, and I
ought not to have said anything about it. However, I will
try and see if I can coax him."

Hera smiled gently, and took her hand, and said, "Do
try, my dear, and don't be angry with the boy. I am sure
he will be a good boy, and do what his mother asks him."

So they went out into the orchard, and there they found
Cupid playing with young Ganymede, a boy whom Zeus
had taken a fancy to, and so had sent his eagle which
caught him up into the skies and brought him to Olympos
to be his cup-bearer at table. They were playing for golden
dice. Cupid was holding his hand full of the dice close to
his breast, and laughing at Ganymede, who was then cast-
ing the last two, with gloomy looks; for he did not like los-
ing. He lost them too, and went off in the sulks, without
noticing the goddesses. Then Aphroditê said:

"You rogue, have you cheated the innocent child? Shame
upon you!—Come now, do something for me, like a good
boy, and I will give you a beautiful ball, the one which
Zeus played with in his cave, when he was a baby. A golden
ball, with blue circles round it! If you throw it up, it
leaves a flaming track in the sky, like a comet! That is
what I will give you, if you will shoot one of your arrows
at Medeia, and make her love Jason."

"Give it me now!" he cried, and dropped his golden
dice on the ground. "Now, now!" and he clutched hold of
her dress on both sides, and clung to her. She smiled at
him, and kissed him, and said:

"No, not now, but I promise to give it as soon as you
have shot one arrow at Medeia."

Without another word the boy slung his quiver across
his shoulder, and caught up his bow, and away he ran;
through the orchard, out of the gates of Olympos, down

through the air, until he saw the earth stretched beneath him, the sea spread wide, and the mountains rising into the sky.

XXII. *Jason and Medeia*

Meanwhile, the heroes were taking counsel together, what was best to do. And Jason said to them, "My friends, it is always best to try persuasion first. Gentle words have great power. Let me go with one or two others, and let us take the sons of Phrixos to be our guides, and open the matter with King Aiêtês. If he will not listen, we can discuss whether it will be well to use force."

So Jason left the ship, with his comrades, and he held in his hand the wand that Hermês had given him, to show that his errand was peaceful. They passed over a plain, with lines of willows, on which was a strange sight. The Colchians are a wild race of men; and when a man dies, they do not bury him, or burn him, but they wrap up the body in an ox-hide, and hang it up in a tree. So in these trees were hanging long rows of bundles, in which were the bodies of their dead.

Then the heroes came to the King's palace, and a wonderful place it was. The god Hephaistos built it, with walls and towers and roomy chambers; and in the courtyard he built four fountains, one running with milk, one with wine, one with fragrant oil, one with water, which grew warm at the setting of the Pleiadês, and at their rising, it became cold as ice. He also made for him bulls with feet of brass, and mouths of brass, who breathed fire out of their jaws; and a great plough of adamant, all in one piece.

Medeia saw them coming. She was there in the company of her sister, the wife of Phrixos, and she cried aloud when she saw Jason with his friends. And the mother lifted up her hands, and cried out, and ran up to embrace her sons; and sobbing, she said:

"So you did not go far, my boys, and here you are back again! Why did you leave your mother?"

Meanwhile Cupid passed unseen, and glided close by Jason. He put arrow to bowstring, and drew it, and shot straight at Medeia, who stood gazing at Jason. The arrow went deep into her heart, like a burning flame, and filled her with amazement, until her soul melted; and from that moment there was only one thought in her, the love for Jason.

That night there was a banquet, and King Aiêtês questioned his guests as to their coming. The eldest son of Phrixos answered: "My lord, our ship was wrecked, and we were saved by this stranger, who has come on a useless quest. His ship was built by the goddess Athena, and no storms can hurt it; and he is sent by one Pelias, who wishes to lay the ghost of Phrixos, by asking the gift of the Golden Fleece. Be it as you will, for they do not offer force, although the ship is full of the chief heroes of Hellas."

This filled the King with fury, and he cried out, "Begone, you traitors! It is my throne you want, and that is why you have brought all these armed men into my house! If you had not tasted my food, and so become my guests, I would have cut out your tongues, and cut off your hands, and left you only your feet to run away!"

The young man would have answered angrily, but Jason checked him, and said, "My lord, bear with us. We have no such desires; for who would cross the wide seas for another man's goods? Fate has sent us, and the bidding of a presumptuous King. Great is your power, and your name shall be published abroad in all Hellas."

These gentle words calmed the King, but he brooded hate and suspicion all the same. However, he thought he might try what these heroes could do, so he said:

"I bear no grudge against brave men, least of all if they have the blood of the gods in their veins. I will give you the Golden Fleece, when I have tried you. I will ask you to do only what I can do myself. I have two bulls, with brazen feet, and brazen mouths, who breathe fire out of their mouths. These bulls I yoke, and plough the fields of Arês; and into the furrows I cast not seed, but teeth from the Theban dragon, which Athena gave me when the dragon was killed by Cadmos. Then a crop of armed men grows up, and as they rise against me, I kill them all. If you can yoke the bulls, and plough the field, and kill the crop of armed men, I will give you the Golden Fleece. If not, I will keep it, for it is not right that a brave man should yield to a coward."

Jason was abashed by this; he did not know what to say; and the King sat, smiling grimly at him. At last he made answer, "My lord, you set me a hard task. But I accept the contest, even though it be my doom to die. Necessity brought me here, and I must do my part."

So he went away with his friends; and Medeia watched him as he went, and her soul crept after him like a dream, for she was possessed now of this terrible passion, and could think of nothing but Jason. But when the heroes were by themselves, the son of Phrixos said, "There is one thing that can help us. There is a maiden here who knows all manner of drugs and spells; if she would help us, we might succeed. I will ask my mother to entreat her." Jason said, "Very well then, go and try; but it is a pitiful thing that we must depend on the help of women." So far he had not noticed Medeia, and did not know who she was. Meanwhile the King laid his plans, so that when the bulls should have killed Jason, he would attack the heroes and kill them, and burn the ship Argo to ashes.

But Medeia had no rest for love of Jason. And after restless sleep, and bad dreams, she got up to seek her sister for comfort. As she opened the door, there on the threshold her sister stood, also in distress, and she cried, "Medeia, what is the matter? Why do you weep so?"

Medeia shrank from telling her secret; she said, "Sister, I have had terrible dreams. I fear the King may be plotting against your sons, along with the strangers!"

The sister said, "Ah me, I am afraid too! But first swear to help me, and to tell no one what I shall say."

Medeia said, "I swear to keep all secret, and to help as far as I can."

Then her sister said, "Can you think of any way to win the contest, for the sake of my sons? I have left them in my chamber, come to pray for help."

Medeia's heart leapt for joy. "I love you, my sister," she said, "and your sons; I will find out a charm to conquer the bulls."

And so Medeia prepared to keep her promise. She could see that disgrace would fall upon her, and perhaps death, for taking the stranger's part against her own father; but she could not help it, for she was filled with an overpowering passion, sent from the gods, like that terrible passion which seized Helen in later days, and brought the ruin of Troy, and the death of thousands of brave men. She could think only of one thing, how to help Jason, although she spoke of her sister and the sons of her sister. She opened her casket of drugs, and took out a wonderful root, called the root of Prometheus; because it grew up from the ground where the eagle had let fall a drop of blood from his liver, or rather, a drop of that fluid which runs in the veins of the gods, for they have not blood like men. If a man should anoint his body with this, for one day he would be safe against any blow from anything made of brass, and safe from fire.

XXIII. *The Brazen Bulls and the Dragon's Teeth*

When day dawned, Medeia put on a beautiful robe, and a veil over it, shining like silver; and calling her twelve maids, she said, "Make ready the mule-car, and come with me to the shrine of Hecatê." They put the mules to, and Medeia mounted the car, and took up the reins and whip, and trotted down the street. The maidens trussed up their skirts, and laid hold of the car six on each side, and ran along with it. So they came to the shrine of Hecatê, goddess of night, lady of spells and charms and potions. Then Medeia said to the maidens, "Listen to me. You saw the stranger, and you know what he has come for. My sister and her sons beg me to accept his gifts, and protect him against the brazen bulls. I have summoned him to meet me here; and you shall have a good share of what he gives." The maidens were pleased to agree to this, and were ready to take part with their mistress.

Meanwhile the sons of Phrixos had returned to Jason, and told him to meet Medeia at the shrine of Hecatê; led by them, Jason came to the tryst, and Medeia saw him come. She sent her maidens apart, and Jason advanced alone.

Never was there so noble a young man as Jason. As Medeia gazed at him, her knees trembled, and she could not address him: they stood face to face speechless.

At last, Jason said, "Maiden, why do you fear me so

much? I am not a man of violence; I come in friendship to this holy place, as your suppliant, to crave your help. For surely one so lovely as you are, must be full of gentle courtesy."

Her heart grew warm within her, and melted like dew upon a rose. She said, "Take heed what I say. When the day for your trial is fixed, and my father has given you the dragon's teeth to sow, on the midnight before bathe in the river, alone; and then put on a black robe, and dig a pit, and there sacrifice a ewe to Hecatê, pouring out before her a pot of honey. Then go away without looking back, no matter what noises you hear. At dawn, soak this root which I give you in water, strip, and anoint your whole body with the water, as if with oil, and sprinkle it over your shield and sword. Then for one day no fire can hurt you, and no strokes from the spears of earth-born men. One thing more: when you have ploughed the soil, and sown the seed, and the earth-born men spring up, cast among them a large stone; they will fight for it together, and kill each other. Then you may take away the Golden Fleece, and may happiness go with you, wherever you go." Then she took courage, and caught hold of his right hand, and said, "Remember me, when you come to your own land, and I will remember you, in despite of my father. If you forget me, may a messenger-bird come over the sea and tell me; and may I be wafted through the air, as an unexpected guest, to remind you how I helped you to escape!" So she said, with tears running down her cheeks. And Jason replied, "Speak not of birds and unexpected guests! If you will come with me, you shall be honoured in all Hellas, and if you will be my wife, only death shall part us."

Then Medeia was glad, but she was unhappy too, for she foresaw that troubles were to come.

And so they parted. Jason returned to his friends, and Medeia passed through her maidens, and saw none of them; she mounted her car, and drove home, and walked through the company, and past her sister, without seeing anyone; she sat down by her bed, with her heart full of thoughts.

The time came. Jason did as he had been told, and anointed himself and his weapons, and in the morning he was ready. King Aiêtês was in full armour, and handed to Jason the helmet with the dragon's teeth; and they repaired to the spot. There the King plumped down the plough in front of Jason, and said with a laugh, "There is your task, my good man! Get on with it!"

Then Jason set up his spear in the ground by a tree, and leaned his helmet against it, and slung his sword over his shoulder; but he bore no armour upon his body, only took the shield with him, as he examined the tracks of the bulls in the soil, and went to meet them. Both bulls rushed out of their lair together, breathing fire and smoke. Jason held his shield before him, to meet their attack; they struck it with their mighty horns, but could not move him. Then he caught one bull by the horn, and dragged it to the yoke, and struck its brazen leg with his foot, and forced it down on the knee. He forced down the other bull beside it, then threw down his shield, and held them both on their fore-knees, while two of his comrades passed him the yoke. He fastened both bulls to the yoke, and lifting the brazen pole between them made it fast. Then Jason slung his shield behind his back, and took up the helmet with the teeth, and his own spear, which he used to prick the sides of the bulls, and to drive them along.

The bulls bellowed, and spouted flame, but it was of no use: go they must, and they drew the great plough, and cut a deep furrow behind them. As they went, Jason dropped the dragon's teeth in the furrow, turning round ever and anon to see whether the earthborn men should rise too soon. But the time was not yet. The field was ploughed; he loosed the oxen, and let them go, while he filled the helmet with water from the river, and quenched his thirst.

By this time, the crop began to appear: helmets and shining spears thrust up from the ground, and soon the men were ready to fight. Then Jason took up a great stone, and hurled it amongst them. The earth-born men yelled, and rushed together, fighting over the stone; and Jason rushed on them, hewing them down, some with head and shoulders above the ground, some half risen to the air, some just standing upright, or making their first rush to battle. He cut them down as you cut corn with a sickle; and there they lay, biting the earth with their teeth.

XXIV. *The Golden Fleece*

But King Aiêtês did not keep his word. He would not give up the Golden Fleece, and he pondered in his mind how he could destroy the heroes and their ship. Medeia was plunged in trouble, to think what must come next; and in the night, she went secretly to the shore, and called out to her kinsmen, "Save me, and save yourselves, while there is yet time, before the King can get his men together. I will charm the serpent, and I will help you to get the Golden Fleece."

So she guided the ship to the place where the fleece hung, in the sacred grove of Arês. She led Jason to the huge oak tree upon which it was hung. As they came near, the serpent, which never slept, saw them with his keen eyes, and hissed loudly at them, wreathing his coils all about. And Medeia sang a soft song, and while she sang, the serpent's head drooped and nodded, and his coils relaxed; while she sang she sprinkled his eyes with her magical brew, and he let his jaw sink down, and slept. Then she smeared ointment upon his head, while Jason took down the Golden Fleece, heavy and thick, and draped it over his left shoulder.

What joy there was in the ship, when they saw Jason return, bearing the Golden Fleece! He led Medeia to a seat in the stern, and said:

"Now, men, for the homeward voyage! Let a part of you row, and the rest hold their shields along the sides, to protect us from the shafts of our enemies."

By this time, Medeia's flight was known, and the people saw that the ship Argo was gone from her moorings. The King came into the market-place, holding a torch, and called upon all to give chase. So they manned their ships, and launched into the river; but the ship Argo was now well on her way.

It would be too long to tell of their journey home. It would be very puzzling too, for the earth must have had an odd shape in those days, as you will see. They came in due time to the mouth of the Danube: and while they were there one of the Colchian ships caught them up. The other ships had gone in different directions, and lost them altogether, but this ship was commanded by Apsyrtos, Medeia's own brother, and it was full of fighting men. This was the cause of a dreadful crime, for which Jason and Medeia paid heavily. They arranged a meeting with Apsyrtos, in order to make peace together; and when Apsyrtos came to the meeting, Jason killed him with his sword. The Argonauts then set upon the Colchians, unexpectedly, and destroyed them.

After this, storms fell upon the heroes, and they would never have got home, but for the speaking stem which Athena had put in the bows of the ship. This stem uttered a voice and spoke, and told them that Jason and Medeia must be purified from the murder by the witch Circê, who lived in the far west in an island.

Then they passed into the Danube, and rowed up the stream, until after a long time they passed from the Danube into the Rhone, and from the Rhone into the Rhine, and from the Rhine into the Ocean Stream, which encompasses the earth all around. Then they came into the quicksands and marshs of the African coast, and into a lake from which they could not get out. Still they endured, and carried the ship Argo on their shoulders over the sand, twelve days and twelve nights. When they came to the sea again, they still had dangers to meet, Scylla and Charybdis, and the Sirens, whom I cannot tell you about now, but at last they found Circê's island, and Circê purified them from the murder.

While Jason was away, Pelias had killed his old father; for he never expected Jason to return, and never meant to keep his promise, and make Jason King. Jason was very angry at this, as you may imagine, and asked Medeia to punish the treachery of Pelias.

So Medeia spoke to the daughters of Pelias in a friendly way. "What a pity it is," she said, "that your father is such an old man, and cannot enjoy his kingdom!" "Well," said they, "it cannot be helped, can it?" "Can it not!" said Medeia. "I will show you." She got an old ram, and cut it up, and boiled it in a cauldron with some of her magical drugs, and sang charms about it, and lo and behold, out of the cauldron skipped a young lamb!

So she persuaded them to kill old Pelias, and boil him too. But no young Pelias came out of the cauldron; he was dead and done for.

Then the son of Pelias banished Jason and Medeia to Corinth.

But still trouble did not leave them. Medeia had been maddened by Cupid's arrow, as you have heard, and Jason seems to have been infected by her madness. He was at first, as you know, a man of peace, and gentle, and just, and not willing to shed blood if he could help it. He also had fine manners, as he showed by helping what seemed to be an ugly old crone. But he was now cruel, and heartless too. He became tired of Medeia, and married another wife. Medeia then destroyed the new wife by her magic, and killed her own two sons, and fled in an air-chariot drawn by dragons to Athens. In Athens she married the old king, and we shall hear of her fate later, when we come to the story of Theseus.

PART 4

XXV. *Theseus and the Robbers*

There is another hero of many great deeds, who was as famous as Heraclês; and that is Theseus. He was the great hero of the Athenians, and he became their king; but first I must tell you of his young days.

Athens lies on the north side of a gulf of the sea, which separates the two parts of Greece on the eastern side, as the Gulf of Corinth does on the western side; between these two gulfs is a neck of land joining the two parts of Greece, called the Isthmus of Corinth.

On the south side of this gulf, opposite Athens, is a strip of land close to the sea, on which was a small city called Troizen; behind it rise the mountains, and behind the mountains is the plain of Argos, with its three mighty fortresses, which I have told of before. In the gulf of the sea, between Athens and Troizen, are many islands; the chief of these islands were famous in Greek history, namely, Aegina and Salamis.

Now the King of Athens, named Aigeus, happened to visit this little city of Troizen, on his travels. He was anxious to have a son, and he had been to consult the oracle of God on that matter, when he came to Troizen, and the King of Troizen entertained him. But the King of Troizen had a beautiful daughter, named Aithra, and King Aigeus fell in love with her, and married her secretly, for he was not quite safe on his throne. His brother had fifty sons, and he had none; so he feared their enmity. By and by he went back to Athens, but he left Aithra behind. When he left her, he said:

"My wife, if you bear a son, bring him up well, and when he is old enough, send him to me at Athens."

She said, "How shall I know when he will be old enough?"

Then King Aigeus said, "See here," and he lifted up a great piece of rock, for he was a strong man, "see here: I lay under this rock my sword and my shoes, which I wear on my feet. When the boy shall be strong enough to lift this rock, let him take my sword and my shoes, and bring them to me, and I shall be able to know him by that sign."

Then he bade her farewell, and went away. And then he forgot all about her.

In due time a boy was born, and they called his name Theseus. Aithra and her father brought him up, and taught him to be strong and brave and wise; for her father was a wise man, so wise that some of his sayings used to be repeated by the Greeks in later ages. One was a very simple saying, but very sensible, and it showed that he was a just man when he might have been unjust: it was this—

Give your servants all their pay;
Keep your word, without delay.

Theseus became strong and healthy in body, and in particular he learnt all the art of wrestling, which proved useful to him by and by. Both in wrestling and in all he did, he depended not on brute force, but on skill and intelligence. His mother did not tell him who his father was, but brought him up quietly in their little town.

Heraclês himself once passed that way, and paid them a visit. He walked up, clad in his lion-skin, and at this sight, everybody else ran away except Theseus. He thought it was a lion, walking on its hind legs, but he was not afraid; boy as he was, he picked up a thick stick, and ran at the lion.

Then Heraclês laughed, and said, "Don't kill me, my good boy! I won't hurt you."

Theseus stopped in surprise, and asked, "Then who are you?"

Heraclês said, "Did you never hear my name? I am Heraclês, and this is the skin of a lion which I once killed, when I was not much older than you."

Theseus was delighted, and they made great friends;

Heraclês told him his own story, and Theseus made up his mind that he would do things like that when he should grow up, but he said nothing about it to the other.

Thus time went on, until he became sixteen years of age. At that age it was proper to cut off his long hair, and make it sacred to some god, as the boys used to do when they became men. Theseus cut off only the front part of his hair, and dedicated it to Apollo, leaving the rest as it was. He must have let his hair grow again, for thus it is in all his pictures; but some warriors of that day used to keep the front of their heads shaven, so that their enemies might not be able to catch hold of it in battle. They shaved off their beards too, for the same reason: it would not be pleasant in the midst of battle, if some one caught you by the beard, and pulled you down. They left the hair growing behind—why, do you think? Because they did not expect to run away.

And now Aithra thought she would tell Theseus who his father was; although she felt anxious, because he seemed to have forgotten all about her, and never sent to enquire how she was doing, and whether he had a son or no. She took Theseus to the rock, and said, "You are quite a man now, my son: try if you can lift up that rock." Then she pointed out the rock, all overgrown in the moss and weeds.

Theseus tried, and he found it a very heavy rock; at first he could not move it, but at last he gave a great heave, and up it came.

"Why, what's this!" he cried. "A sword and a pair of shoes!"

"Your father's sword and shoes," said Aithra; and as he gazed at her in astonishment, she went on, "Your father is King of Athens, over on the other side of the sea. He left us here for good reasons of his own, and told me, that when you were strong enough to lift that rock, you were to put on the shoes, and sling the sword over your shoulder, and go to him at Athens."

"And what then?" said Theseus.

"I don't know what he means to do with you," she replied. "Perhaps you will be king too, but in any case, you must do what he tells you. I will get a ship, and send you across."

"No, no," said Theseus, "no ship: what do the shoes mean? They mean I must walk; and the sword means I must fight my way."

"Oh," said Aithra, "don't do that, my boy! The road is full of robbers and bloodthirsty men, who are much too strong for you, my boy!"

But he cried out, "Robbers! Then I will kill them, like Heraclês!"

This made Aithra very sad, and she did her best to persuade him not to go by land; but all in vain, and go he would.

So he thanked his mother, and his good grandfather, for their kindness, and prepared for the journey. He put on a tunic of deep crimson, and a leathern bonnet, and slung his father's sword over his left shoulder; with the shoes on his feet, and a thick woollen mantle, and a couple of lances in his left hand, he set out on the path, which was to lead him through a long life of noble deeds, until he came to be honoured like Heraclês.

He took the road into the hills; and he had not gone far, before a huge giant rushed out at him, brandishing a thick club. Theseus, who knew all the tricks of boxing and wrestling, laid down his lances, and let him come up; then he lightly stepped aside, and caught the giant's right arm and twisted it, so that he let fall the club. In a trice Theseus picked up the club, and brought it down on the giant's head, and that was the end of him. You see he had made a good beginning to his journey. He took the club along with him, in case it might be useful.

That night he slept in the woods, breathing the sweet smell of pine-trees; and next morning he walked on to the isthmus. But there on his road he saw another giant robber, named Sinis. They called him the Pine-bender, for he was so strong, that he could catch a pine-tree by the top, and bend it down to the ground. When strangers came that way, he used to say, "Please help me with this pine-tree"; and as soon as the stranger had got his arms round the top of the tree, Sinis used to laugh, and let go, and the pine-tree used to spring up, and shoot off the man like a stone from a catapult. Or he would pull down two trees, and would fasten the man one arm and one leg to each, and then let the trees go. This used to tear the man in half, so people said. Theseus no doubt had heard about Sinis; so when Sinis came up smiling, and asked his help to bend down a tree. Theseus gave him a tap on the head with the club, which stunned him. Then he pulled down two pine-trees, and tied their tops down; he fastened Sinis between them, and let the tops go, and so Sinis was treated as he used to treat strangers.

As Theseus went on, he met a savage wild sow, which gave him some trouble; but he ran his lance through her, and then finished her off with his sword.

All this happened on the level ground, but now the ground began to rise, until the way became only a narrow path leading round a high cliff, half-way up the side. As he came round a bend, he saw in front of him a small piece of flat ground, with grass growing upon it, and a spring of fresh water bubbling out; and in the middle was a huge man, looking wild and fierce, sitting upon a seat, with a large basin full of water at his feet.

"Who are you, stranger?" said he.

"And who are you?" said Thescus.

"I am Sciron," said the other. "And now, who are you?"

Theseus said, "I am a traveller, on the way to Athens."

"Ha!" said the man. "I hope you may get there! But that depends upon me. No traveller may pass me, without paying toll."

"What is the toll?" said Theseus.

"To wash my feet," said the robber.

"What!" said Theseus. "I, a free man, to do the work of a slave!"

"If you do not," said Sciron, "look down the cliff, and see what will become of you."

Theseus looked down the cliff, and at the bottom what should he see but a huge tortoise, looking up at the cliff with gaping mouth; and well he might, for that was where his food came from. Sciron, you see, used to make travellers wash his feet, and if they would not, then he kicked them over the cliff. But if they did wash his feet, he kicked them down all the same, only he did not tell Theseus that. Theseus saw the huge tortoise, and he noticed a great quantity of bones lying about, so he could easily guess what happened. However, he pretended to be frightened, and turned back to the bowl.

"Very well," he said, "I suppose I must. But, sir, this water will never do to wash your noble feet. It is full of dirt, let me get you some more," and without waiting for an answer, he tilted up the bowl and let the water run out, and then he picked up the bowl, and brought it down with a crash on Sciron's head. Sciron fell down half-dazed, and Theseus kicked him over the cliff; as he looked down he could see the huge tortoise joyfully waddling up, and gnawing the flesh off the robber's bones. But the tortoise did not know that he would never get another meal of that sort.

Theseus had earned a rest now, and that night he slept in the robber's own cave, which he saw in the side of the rock. There was plenty of food there, and all he wanted.

Next day, he passed out of the dangerous path, and walked over hill and dale, until he came to another fertile spot. Here he found a fourth robber, who was not such a savage as the others. At least, he gave the travellers a chance, for he used to challenge them to a wrestling match. You may imagine that this suited Theseus quite well. He hung up his sword on a tree, and he leaned his club and his lances against it; then he stripped for the bout. The robber had no art or skill in his wrestling, but Theseus knew all the tricks of the ring, as I have told you. The robber stepped up cautiously, spreading his arms wide, to get a grip as far outside his enemy as he could; but Theseus quickly stepped in, with his hands close together. He got his left arm over the robber's neck, so that he held the robber's head tight under his left armpit, and with his right hand he got hold of the robber's body from underneath; then he gave a great heave, and threw him backwards over his own head, the throw that wrestlers call the Flying Mare. The robber fell on his head, and broke his neck.

Theseus was now near Athens, and only one more robber was left to deal with, who lived on the last hill before you come to Athens by the shore-path. This robber was named Procrustês, the Hammerer. It was evening as

Theseus drew near, and he saw Procrustês sitting at the door of his home. Procrustês called out:

"Welcome, stranger, may I offer you a bed for the night?"

"I thank you," said Theseus. "I should be very glad of a bed; it is evening, and I have had a long day."

"Well," said Procrustês, "come in, and take your choice."

That sounded an odd way of speaking, but Theseus came in, and there he saw two beds, one very long, and one very short.

"I do not know, really," said Theseus. "The small one seems too short for me, but I should not like to deprive you of yours."

"Ha ha!" said Procrustês. "You need not worry—I can make you fit either of them!" and roaring with laughter, he took up a saw in one hand, and a hammer in the other. "All I do is, to put long men on the short bed, and saw off the ends that stick out; and I put short men on the long bed, and hammer out their legs till they fit!" He roared with laughter again.

But you understand that Theseus was not so simple as he seemed. He had been watching all this time, and now with a quick leap, he had hold of the robber's right hand and arm, which he twisted in his clever way, and made him drop the hammer. Then Theseus picked up the hammer, and hammered out Procrustês on his own bed, until his life departed from him.

XXVI. *Theseus and Medeia*

But rumour runs fast, and it came to Athens. The people were all summoned by sound of trumpet, and when they met in the market-place, there was Aigeus, the king. The spokesman of the people lifted up his voice, and said:

"My lord, why did the trumpet call us together? Is there danger of war: are bands of robbers lifting the cattle and sheep? Or what trouble is there?"

The king said, "A messenger has come from the Isthmus, who tells of prodigious deeds done by a mighty man. Sinis the Pine-bender is dead; the wild sow is dead, which killed men and laid waste the country-side; Sciron lies at the foot of his cliff; the wrestling-school of Cercyon is shut up for good; Procrustês has been hammered on his own bed."

The spokesman said, "Who is the man, sir, who does these mighty deeds? For such things are not done without God's help. Is he alone, or at the head of an army?"

The King said, "He has a couple of servants with him, so I am told; he wears a crimson tunic and a leathern headpiece upon his nut-brown hair; he carries two lances and a club, a sword with ivory hilt is slung over his shoulder, and a woollen mantle covers all."

The people dispersed, and welcomed Theseus in crowds along the way; and the king made a banquet to do him honour. He had forgotten all about Aithra, and never knew who Theseus was; but his wife the queen was Medeia, whom you have heard of already, a beautiful and terrible witch, and she knew him at once by her magical power.

But she bided her time; and by and by she said to the King, "Who is this young man?" He said, "I don't know, but he is a fine fellow." Medeia said, "Yes, indeed he is. He has destroyed all those robbers, and the wild sow; why not send him after the bull of Marathon?" For at Marathon, not far from Athens, was the Cretan bull, which, as you remember, Heraclês had brought there from Crete; and this bull was doing a great deal of damage. Medeia hoped that the bull would kill Theseus, and then her own son might be King when Aigeus died.

Aigeus agreed, and Theseus set off for Marathon, with a strong rope to bring back the bull. He made a noose in this rope, and laid a plan to tackle the bull; for, as you remember, he did his great deeds by cleverness, not by brute force. I do not know exactly how he managed it; but the picture which the Greeks made shows him lying under the bull, so I suppose he did something like what the Spanish bull-fighters do. He took off his crimson tunic, and carried it bundled up in one hand, holding the noose in the other. Then he walked quietly up to the bull, and as the bull stood pawing the ground, and preparing to charge, he spread out the red cloth suddenly towards the left, fluttering in the air. This caught the bull's eye, for they hate red cloth, and as he moved his head towards the red cloth, Theseus threw it down, and dived under him on the near side, and got the noose over his hind legs; then he pulled the noose tight, and there was the bull, caught fast. Theseus brought the bull back to Athens, and it was killed at a solemn sacrifice.

Thus Medeia's first plan was foiled; but she made a second plot, to poison Theseus. She kept on dropping hints, and talking to Aigeus, and pretending she feared that the young man might plot against the King; he was so popular in the city, she said, that he might lead the people to rebel against him; it would be impossible now to send him away, and the only thing was, to poison him. Aigeus did not like this plan, but he was persuaded by his wicked wife, and at last he agreed.

So the next time they were dining together, Medeia put poison in the wine-cup, and handed it to Theseus. But just as Theseus lifted the cup to his lips, Aigeus happened to notice the sword which was slung over his shoulder. He had never seen it so close before, and when he saw it, he knew it as his own. At once he dashed the cup from the lips of Theseus, and cried out, "You are my son!" Then Theseus showed him the sword, and the shoes, which Aigeus had never looked at before, and told him the whole story. Aigeus was very much ashamed that he had neglected his son so long, but he was much more glad that he had been saved from murdering him. He was very angry with Medeia, and banished her from the country, and Theseus was acknowledged as his true son and heir. Although Aigeus was still afraid of his brother and his brother's fifty sons, Theseus was safe enough, because all the people loved him and admired him.

XXVII. *Theseus and the Minotaur*

But Theseus had not done with bulls; and his last fight was the most terrible of all. The bull of Marathon, you remember, had been brought from Crete by Heraclês; and he left a son behind him in Crete, who was half bull and half man, named the Minotaur, which means the bull of Minos, King of Crete. Minos made a pet of this bull, as he had done with the sire, and he had a wonderful house built for it. There was a very clever man living in Crete, named Daidalos, an architect and an inventor, who could make houses, and statues, and all sorts of machines such as people had then; in fact, they say his statues could even walk. Daidalos built a house for the Minotaur, which was called the Labyrinth; it was a maze full of winding passages, like the maze of Hampton Court, only more mazy still, and all of stone; the paths led to a cave in the middle, where the Minotaur slept. But most horrible of all, this monster was fed with the flesh of men, who were turned into the Labyrinth. Once in, they soon lost their way, and kept wandering about; but the Minotaur knew all the ways, and it gave him sport to hunt them until he caught them, and killed them, and ate them up.

Now Minos had had a quarrel with the city of Athens, because his son had been killed there, perhaps by accident, perhaps not. This son had been victorious in the Athenian games, and had gone afterwards to tackle the bull of Marathon, which came from Crete as you remember, and the bull had killed him—at least, that was one story. But Minos made war on King Aigeus in consequence, and forced him to pay a tribute every year, but not a tribute of money; he was forced to send to Minos every year seven young men and seven young maidens, whom Minos turned into the Labyrinth for the Minotaur to eat. This was more bitter for Aigeus than all his other fears and anxieties.

The time was now come for the tribute to be paid: and lots were to be cast for the young men and maidens. Then Theseus spoke out boldly:

"Father, it is a shameful thing to send these boys and girls to be cruelly killed by a monster. Let me go with them, and I will kill the beast!"

All were astonished, Aigeus was dismayed, but Theseus stuck to it; go he would, never would he put up with this cruel tribute. And like a true leader of men, he would never command one of his subjects to do anything which he was not ready to do himself. So the lots were cast for the others, and they went down in a sad procession, to the place where the ship lay that was to take them to Crete. Minos was on board the ship himself.

Now this ship bore a black sail, in token of mourning; and King Aigeus on parting gave Theseus a white sail, with the words, "My son, if God makes you able to destroy the monster, put up this white sail on your return, that I may see it far away on the water, and know that my son is safe." This Theseus promised to do.

The ship set sail: a fair breeze from the north blew it over the waters. On board were Theseus and the other victims, unarmed and helpless, for such was the will of Minos; and Minos himself looked at them, gloating with joy. He even put out his hand, and rudely stroked the cheeks of one of the maidens, who cried out, "Help me, Theseus!"

Then Theseus rolled his dark eyes in anger, and said, "Son of Zeus, that is not lawful; you have dropped the rudder of your mind. Hold back your violent hand! God's destiny rules all, and what he has decreed, the scales of justice shall weigh out for us. That fate we shall fulfil, when it comes; until then, hold your harsh purpose. If Zeus was your father, I am akin to Poseidon, and indeed I may call him father, and the nymphs of the sea gave my mother a golden veil at her wedding. Therefore control yourself, for I would not care to see the light of day if you should do violence to one of this company. Before that, we two will come to a trial of strength, and destiny shall decide between us."

The sailors were amazed to hear these bold words. Minos had no will to try his strength with the invincible wrestler; but he thought of a new plan, and cried out, "Zeus, my father, give me a sign with thy lightning! And you, if you are akin to Poseidon, the Earth-shaker, dive down to his abode, and bring me back this ring that glistens on my hand! Now you shall see if the lord of thunder hears my prayer!"

At these words the lightning flashed; and Minos threw the ring into the sea, and said, "Look now at the clear sign of Zeus; into the sea with you, and Poseidon will give you fame over all the earth."

Theseus was not afraid; he stood up on the stern, and dived down into the sea out of sight. The steersman would have brought up the ship to await him, but Minos would not allow it; he called out, "Keep her before the wind," in hope that if Theseus did come up again, he might be left behind to drown. Little did he know the counsels of the gods! So the ship sped on before the wind, and the young Athenians shuddered and wept at their coming fate, and the loss of their champion.

But the champion was quite safe. As soon as he dived beneath the surface, a pair of dolphins caught him up, one under each arm, and carried him down and down through the water, clear as crystal, with a delicate tinge of green; among the shoals of fishes, which stared at them with great round eyes, through the seaweeds, to a coral cave, where the daughters of the sea used to dwell. Their radiant forms shone with splendour like fire through soft transparent robes, like silvery muslin, and golden bands were round their heads. They were all dancing gracefully in the coral cave.

There he saw the Queen of the Sea, Amphitritê, who threw about him a purple robe, and set a wreath of dark red roses upon his head. She said:

"Why have you come, my boy?"

Theseus answered, "To fetch the ring of King Minos, who has just thrown it into the sea."

The nymphs had ceased dancing, when he came in; and now one of them glided up—they do not need to walk; they can glide up, or down, or all along, whenever they will, as swift as a tunny-fish: and she held out the ring to Theseus, saying, "Here it is. I caught it as he threw."

They delayed him no longer. The dolphins took him back between them, far swifter than a ship, and brought him up on the ship's quarter, where he appeared to the amazement of the whole company, and the secret wrath of Minos. And, most wonderful of all, when he emerged from the sea, and stood once more on the deck, to return his ring to Minos, Theseus was quite dry. See what wonders the gods can do!

Now they came to the Cretan haven; and now the great procession marched up from the haven to the city, with the fourteen young men and maidens in their midst, sad and mournful; but the city was full of rejoicing, for there was a feast to celebrate this tribute and this sacrifice to the terrible Minotaur. The whole road, three miles long, was

thronged with people in gay clothes, shouting and waving
their hands, as you can see to-day in the pictures they
made themselves: and the women looked out of the upper
windows of the houses, with bare necks and shoulders
after their country fashion, and with tight bodices and
flounces on their skirts.

Amongst them was Ariadnê, daughter of King Minos,
who with her friends sat on an upper balcony of the king's
palace. "Look," she said, "there are the victims. Poor
things, how sad they look! But who is that marching at
the head of them? He is not sad like the rest—he is proud
and brave, and holds up his head."

One of the ladies-in-waiting said, "Why, that's the
young son of the King of Athens. And what do you think
they say? He was not taken by lot, he came of his own
free will, and says he will fight with the monster."

"Brave boy!" said Ariadnê, "it is a shame he should
die." And she fell silent, and let the others talk; for the
instant she saw Theseus, love struck her heart, and she
determined to help him.

But what could she do? If he killed the monster, he
would never get out of the Labyrinth; and would he kill
him? How could he, without a weapon? You see, she did
not know the story of Theseus, as you do, or how good he
was at wrestling. At last she went to Daidalos, the architect
of the Labyrinth, and asked him how she could help the
young prince to find his way out of the Labyrinth. Daida-
los was very much afraid to meddle, but he was an Athen-
ian himself, and wished well to Theseus. At last he thought
of something that could not easily be found out; and he
said:

"Madam, all that I can do is this. Take this ball of
thread, and convey it to him. Tell him to tie one end to
the post of the door, and to unroll it as he goes; then
if he succeeds in killing the monster, he can roll it up
as he comes out, and nobody will ever know how he
managed."

Ariadnê thanked Daidalos; and that night she sent
her old nurse, with the ball of thread tied in a corner of
her dress. Some say she sent also a sword, but I do not
think she did that, although we often see it in the pictures
of Theseus: it would be difficult for an old woman to hide

a sword, and if she were searched she would be suspected of some mischief, but who would suspect a ball of thread?

The old woman managed somehow to see Theseus; she gave him the ball of thread, and the message, and added, "The princess says that she loves you, and prays you to take her away with you, if you win the fight." "That I will indeed," said Theseus, and they parted.

The procession of youths and maidens came to the Labyrinth. The gates were opened, and they were led in; then the gates were shut. There they stood, helpless and hopeless, for they knew nothing of the ball of thread, and they did not really believe that Theseus would win. But Theseus said:

"Be of good cheer, my friends. God is with us! Did you not see me come out of the water? And now—this place is full of winding ways, and no one who gets in can ever find his way out; so you must stay here, and not stir one step from the gates. Leave the rest to me."

So saying, he drew out the ball of thread from his breast, and tied one end of it to the doorpost; then he moved away into the dark paths, unrolling the thread as he went. The others were all attention, for here was something new, which they did not understand; but it made them hope once more, for hope is always with us—Prometheus did well to put blind hope in our hearts, a more precious thing than knowledge.

So Theseus moved cautiously on, coming now to a blank wall, now to a place with many turnings; and although he tried to keep his direction towards the middle, as true as he could, yet before long he really did not know which way he was going. Well was the place called the maze; it was enough to maze anyone. But at last he came to an open space, where he saw a black cave; and on the floor of the cave lay the monster like a strong giant with the head of a bull, and bull's horns.

Up leapt the monster, and let out a great roar, and rushed at Theseus. What happened then I do not know, for I was not there, and no one was there to see; nor did Theseus tell tales about it afterwards, for he was no boaster, as some of the heroes were. Some of his pictures show him holding a sword; but, as I said before, I do not think he had one, for all the captives were unarmed, and the old nurse brought him none. I am sure that he used all the art of wrestling and boxing, which he knew so well, and that God put strength into his limbs, as he so often does when the weaker man defends the right. It was of no use for Theseus to strike at the bull's head or neck, as he would have done with a man; so he must have struck at the heart, or the mark, or used the wrestler's trippings and grapplings. In the end, the monster was killed.

But there was no time to rest. Theseus offered a prayer of thankfulness, and once more picked up his ball of thread; then he went back by the way he had come, a long round-about, winding up the thread as he went; for he wished to leave no trace to make Minos think that someone had helped him. And you may imagine the joy of his friends, when they saw him return, bruised and covered with blood, but victorious over the horrible monster.

How they got out, I do not know. Perhaps the guards had left the door unlocked, because they never expected anyone to come out alive; perhaps (as I think) the old nurse was there, waiting, for you may be sure Ariadnê was waiting somewhere. But get out they did. It was night; the city was asleep, and the prisoners crept down the long road to the harbour. Somewhere they met Ariadnê, wrapped up so that no one could tell who she was; quietly they climbed into their ship, quietly they hoisted the sail, and before anyone was awake in the morning, the ship was sailing away far over the seas.

I need not tell you of Ariadnê's joy, or the love of Theseus for her kind heart. They were happy together, and when they came to a pleasant island next day, they landed there, and stayed there quite a long time. And they might have lived happily ever after; but it so happened that the goddess Artemis killed her. I do not know why, but Artemis was a hard and cruel goddess, and easily offended. They do say that the god Dionysos then raised her to heaven as his wife, and placed among the stars the crown he gave her at his marriage. Others say that Theseus deserted her, but there are always those who will say unkind things. I think myself he was a noble and true gentleman, and it does not seem like him to desert the girl who saved him. At least what happened next shows that he was very much hurt by her loss; his mind was so troubled that he forgot his promise to his old father, he forgot to put up the white sail to show that he was safe; and the ship came sailing home, with the old black sail hoisted.

Every day King Aigeus would climb the Acropolis hill, which stands in the middle of Athens, and sit there watching the distant sea for his son's ship. He sat on that projecting rock which you can see in front of the great gate; there is a beautiful little temple built on it now, the temple of Wingless Victory, as if the people meant that Victory sat on their hill, and could never fly away. There sat Aigeus; and there one morning he spied a sail. The sun shone upon it, and he could not tell for a long time what colour the sail was; but as the ship drew nearer, he saw it was black. The old man's heart broke, and he fell down from the rock, and died. The sea is still called the Aegean Sea, after King Aigeus, and some believed that he threw himself into the sea; but the sea is some distance from this rocky hill, and I think I have told you the true story. So the people did not go down to the sea to meet the ship, for they thought all was lost: but when Theseus and the young men and maidens came out, and the news ran to their parents, then there was rejoicing and feasting. Only Theseus was sad, for his old father was dead.

XXVIII. *Daidalos and Icaros, and the End of Theseus*

You wonder perhaps what was happening in Crete. Minos was in a great fury when he heard how his Minotaur was dead, and the prisoners escaped. He enquired of everybody, and found out about the ball of thread, and how Daidalos had suggested it; so he took Daidalos and his son Icaros, and shut them up in the Labyrinth which Daidalos had made.

But Daidalos was too clever to be kept in the Labyrinth. And yet how was he to get out? The walls were high, the gates were locked and barred; nothing but a bird could get out. Very well: he determined to be a bird. He was always inventing things. He had invented the saw, amongst other things. He had noticed some one rubbing a snake's jaw, which is all jagged, against a piece of stick, which he soon rubbed through; and the idea came to him that he might make a metal tool like the snake's jaw, with teeth, which cuts easily through wood, when it might take a long time to chop it with an axe. So there was nothing strange when he asked for his tools and his materials; Minos thought he might as well make something useful instead of wasting his time. It seemed likely to be something quite new, as he kept asking for wax and reeds and eagles' feathers.

What do you think Daidalos was making? Wings! He fitted the feathers in proper order along a frame, and fixed them with wax, just as you make the panspipes. Before long he had a fine large pair of wings ready to fit on his arms and shoulders, and a smaller pair for Icaros. He tried them, and flapped about, and after a little practice, he found he could fly almost as well as a bird. Then he taught Icaros; but he warned him to be careful. "As we fly over the sea," he said, "do not fly too low, or you will be drenched by the spray, and the wings will be clogged; and do not fly too high, for if you go near the sun, he will melt you." Icaros promised everything; and then, boy-like, he forgot all about it.

So one fine day, the people of Crete were astonished to see two birds rise from the Labyrinth, huge creatures, bigger than any bird they had seen in their lives before. Then they looked harder, and saw it was Daidalos and his son, flapping away for dear life. They told Minos the news, and great was his rage; but he could do nothing. Away they flew, farther and farther, until they were only dots in the sky; and at last they were seen no more.

Icaros was delighted. He flew steadily at first, but when they had got clear out of sight of the haven, he became excited, and dived about like a real eagle. Down he went almost into the sea, up again higher into the air. "Take care, my boy," cried his father, again and again, but the boy took no notice; higher and higher he went, until he came too close to the sun, and the sun melted the wax, and the feathers fell out of his wings, and he dropped into the sea like a stone. The part where he fell is still called the Icarian Sea.

Daidalos himself escaped to Sicily, and thought he was safe. Minos sailed everywhere with ships of war, to bring

him back, if he could find him; but he did not say what
he wanted; all he did was, wherever he came, to put a
puzzle to those he met. He knew that Daidalos would try
his wits on any puzzle he came across, and he did not
think anyone else would solve his puzzle. This was the
puzzle: he offered a shell, twisted round and round like
a turret staircase, and said, "If anyone can pass a thread
through this shell, I will give him a large reward."

He came at last to the city where Daidalos was, and the
King of the place entertained him. In the course of talk,
Minos said, "Here is a puzzle, my friend; can you thread
this shell?" The King took it and turned it over and over,
and looked wise; at last he said, "Well, if you leave it with
me, I think I can manage it,"—not that he really thought
anything of the kind, but Daidalos was then hiding in his
house, and he thought that if Daidalos could solve the
puzzle, he might get the credit himself.

So Minos left the shell, and the King went straight off
to Daidalos with it. Daidalos looked at it a minute; then
he said, "Find me an ant." The ant was found, and Daidalos
tied a fine thread round the ant; then he bored a hole
in the top of the shell, and put the ant in at the bottom:
the ant tried to escape, and ran straight up the shell, and
round and round the curls of the spiral, and out at the
top, pulling the thread behind him. Daidalos cut the thread,
saying, "Good-bye, ant, and many thanks," and let the
ant go. Then he gave the shell back to the King, with a
thread running right through it, and the King took it to
Minos.

Then Minos said, "I know who did that! No one but
Daidalos could have done it, and you have got him here!
Hand over the man to me, or it shall be the worse for you."
The King was afraid of Minos, and he promised to hand
over Daidalos that night after dinner. But when Minos went
to the bath, before dinner, he was drowned in the bath.
So Daidalos was safe, and I do not think you will feel
very sorry for cruel King Minos.

There is still something left to tell of Theseus, when
he found himself King of Athens after his old father's
death. He had a hard fight to establish himself. His fifty
cousins fought against him, and he was obliged to defend
himself; but in the end he killed all the fifty, and brought

his enemies low. He joined Heraclês in the war against the Amazons, and defeated the Amazons again in Athens itself; for they had invaded Athens, and made their camp on the lower part of the Acropolis hill, a flat rock overlooking the market-place, which is called Areiopagos. In the New Testament it is called Mars' Hill, and it is the place where St. Paul preached a sermon once in Athens. There Theseus defeated this strange tribe of fighting women.

Theseus made a great friend of a man named Peirithoös, and when Peirithoös wanted to carry off Persephonê from the lower world, Theseus helped him. You remember Persephonê, daughter of Demeter, who was carried off by King Hadês and made Queen of the dark world below: Peirithoös thought he would do her a good turn if he carried her off himself, and made her his wife. But it was a great mistake for a mortal man to dare such a thing, and Peirithoös paid dearly for it, as you will hear.

Theseus and Peirthoös got down safely to Tartaros, but Hadês outwitted them. He received them kindly, and bade them be seated; but he made them seat themselves in the Chair of Forgetfulness, cut out of the rock. As they sat down, they forgot all the past; and the arms and sides of the chair grew round them, so that they became part of the rock. There sat Peirithoös, and there he must sit for ever; there also would Theseus have sat for ever, but after a long time Heraclês came down, and brought him away. But Theseus left a bit of his legs sticking to the rock; and they say all the Athenians who were born afterwards had the same bit of their legs wanting, but I have not noticed that in the Athenians I have seen.

When Theseus returned to Athens, he did great things for his city. It was only a small place, and the people lived all over the country in villages; but Theseus collected them together into the city of Athens, and fortified it and made it strong. Thus they could till their farms while there was peace, but when war came, they gathered together into the city to defend themselves. And he appears now and then in the Greek stories: a great King and lawgiver, a friend of those who were in trouble, and one who did good to mankind, like his friend and comrade Heraclês. And there we will leave him.

XXIX. *Meleagros and the Brand*

You remember how Cheiron bade farewell to Jason, and his wife stood by, holding the infant Achillês in her arms. I am now to tell you the story of the child's father, whose name was Peleus. He had many adventures before the boy was born, and one of them was in hunting the Calydonian Boar.

He was one of the Argonauts, who brought back the Golden Fleece, and with him was young Meleagros, the sons of a prince of Calydon in North-western Greece. When Meleagros came home, he found his father's kingdom in confusion. The king had forgotten to make due sacrifice to Artemis, who, as you have heard, was a cruel and hard goddess. To punish the mistake, she sent upon Calydon a monstrous boar, which breathed fire, and destroyed all the crops and stock of the countryside. Meleagros therefore collected a band of friends to encounter this boar; among them was Atalanta, a very man-like young woman. She was a great huntress and fighter. She actually took part in the quest of the Golden Fleece, and now she was eager to join in the new quest. Atalanta was the first to hit the boar with an arrow, then another shot him in the eye, but Meleagros killed him with a blow in the side. Then he gave the skin to Atalanta, because he was in love with her. This enraged the others, who said the skin ought not to be given to a woman; a fight followed, and in the fight Meleagros killed the brothers of Althaia, his mother.

Althaia saw the victorious band returning from the hunt with Atalanta and the spoils of the terrible boar. They went up to the temple to give thanks for their victory; but behind them came the dead bodies of those who had been slain. "Who are these?" cried Althaia; and when she heard who they were, "Who killed them?" Imagine her horror, when she was told that her own son had killed her brothers. Her love for her son turned to hatred, and she remembered a strange event, which happened when the boy was a baby.

Seven days after his birth the Three Fates appeared, and looked at the baby. Then one of the Fates said, in a

128

solemn voice, "This child will live as long as that brand on the hearth shall burn. When it is burnt up, the child will die." Althaia had instantly caught up the brand from the fire, and put it out, and laid it aside carefully in a chest, where she had kept it ever since.

And now she made haste to the chest and unlocked it, and took up the brand and cast it upon the fire. As it burnt, Meleagros in the temple felt as if fire were burning within him, and fell down on the ground: before long the brand was burnt and Meleagros was dead.

When this deed was done, Althaia came to her senses and bitterly repented; but that was of no use, she could not bring her son back to life, and in despair she made away with herself. The young man's sisters wept so much, that even Artemis took pity on them; she touched them with a rod, and turned them into guinea-hens, which cackle all day and all night in a melancholy way. It was no great kindness, you may think, but Artemis meant well, for those who worshipped Artemis took care never to eat guinea-fowl. The sisters went on weeping, and some say their tears turned into drops of amber.

XXX. *Atalanta*

You may like to hear the rest of Atalanta's history before we go on. Her father had wanted a son, and when Atalanta was born, he said, "What's the use of a girl to me? Put her out on the mountains, and let her die." So the servants put her out on the mountains. There a she-bear came along, and took a fancy to the strange little thing, and fed her with her own milk. By and by some hunters passed that way, and found her, and saved her, and brought her up.

She became a hard woman, like her hard father, and like the hard life she was forced to lead. She cared for no hardship, she shrank from no toil, she feared no wild beast of the forest. Even when two terrible Centaurs attacked her, she cared nothing, but killed them both. When she grew up, she found out her father, and came to live in his house. She made a great name for herself, in running and wrestling and other manly sports; she even wrestled with Peleus, and beat him. She must have been a handful to manage; so her father soon became tired of her, and did his best to find a husband who would relieve him of his troublesome daughter. At first she would not hear of a husband; but at last she agreed, on certain conditions.

The conditions were, that if anyone wanted to marry her, he must run a race with her; if he lost the race, he was to lose his life. But she was so beautiful, that many young men were willing to try, even on those terms; many did try, and failed, and they were put to death.

One young man, named Milanion, a fine young fellow, laughed at this. "What fools you are," said he, "to run such a risk for a girl! Are there not plenty of girls in the country? You will not catch me risking my neck for one, no matter how beautiful she may be."

"That is all very well," said the young men, "but you have not seen her. Come with us to the next race, and then you may talk." "All right," he said, "I will come," and he went with them to see the race.

There they stood at the starting-post: Atalanta, like Artemis herself, as beautiful and as hard; and the young man, full of strength and grace, and confident that he would win. Off they went: he was quick on his feet, but nothing to Atalanta, who sped off like the wind, and easily came in first. Then the young man was led off to his death.

But would you believe it? No sooner had Milanion set eyes on Atalanta, than he fell in love as deeply as the rest. He thought he had never seen anything so beautiful as Atalanta, and on the spot he declared that he would try his luck. Atalanta herself was sorry, as she saw this fine young man. "You are only a boy," she said, "and why should you throw your life away? Think how many lives have been wasted already!" For she had grown tired of this; indeed, she thought the condition would have kept men away, and all she wanted was to be left alone. But in fact, she fell a little in love with Milanion too, and she did her best to dissuade him. Why she did not accept him at once, if she liked him, I do not know; but perhaps she felt that it would make her look small before the world, and she did not really love him enough, as yet. So a day was fixed for the new race.

Milanion was not quite so cheerful when he got away. He did not feel so sure he would win; and now that he could not see her, he did not feel so sure she was worth it. But he felt he could not back out of the challenge. Then he prayed to the goddess Aphroditê to help him, and she heard his prayer; for she did not like this hard maiden, who made light of the goddess of love. She had a wonderful tree in her grove, which bore golden apples; three of these apples she picked, and gave them to Milanion, and told him what to do.

The day came. There were crowds of people to see the race: the King was there, with his court; Atalanta was there, girt in a short tunic, like Artemis, and ready to run. Milanion came, with the golden apples tucked into a corner of his tunic. They made rather a bulge, but no one noticed it in all that excitement.

The two runners stood at the starting-point; the signal was given—they were off. Atalanta did not run as swiftly as usual, for her own heart weakened a little, to see this beautiful young man running for his life. For a little time, they ran neck and neck; but the ardour of the race took hold of Atalanta, and she shot ahead.

Then Milanion pulled out one of his apples, and rolled it ahead of Atalanta. She caught sight of the bright thing, and hesitated, and stopped in her course to pick it up. Milanion passed her, and sped away at full speed. But Atalanta tucked her apple into her bosom, and off she went again; she soon passed Milanion, and left him behind her. Now Milanion pulled out another apple, and sent it rolling a little to one side. Once more Atalanta saw the apple, and darted away from the course to pick it up; once more Milanion ran ahead, and this time he gained a good deal of ground.

But the pace was telling on Milanion. He began to pant, and his breath came dry from his throat; run as he would, he could not keep ahead, and now he took out his last apple. This time, he threw it as hard as he could, right away to one side, but so that Atalanta could see it. And as before, Atalanta darted in pursuit, and ran right out of the course until she was able to catch it, and tucked it way with the rest.

They were not yet at the end of the race, and Atalanta

began to gain on Milanion; but Aphroditê was watching, unseen, and she made the apples grow heavier and heavier, until Atalanta felt as if she were carrying a weight of lead in her bosom. She went slower and slower, and Milanion kept ahead, and won the race.

Then there were great rejoicings, and Atalanta was no less pleased than the rest, although she did not say much about it. So they were married, and they deserved to live happily ever after, but unluckily they did not. For they gave offence to Zeus, and he turned them into a pair of lions. Perhaps after all, Atalanta was more happy as a lioness than she would have been as a woman, but we do not know her side of the story, because she could no longer tell it.

XXXI. *Peleus and Thetis*

We return to Peleus, the father of the little boy whom Cheiron's wife held in her arms.

Peleus was the son of Aiacos, Prince of Aegina, who was himself a son of Zeus. Aegina is a very important island in Greek history, and the heroes who were of the family of Aiacos played a great part. Aiacos himself was a just man; so that he was even asked to settle disputes among his kinsmen, the Immortals, and after death, he became one of the Judges of the dead, in the dark house of Hadês.

Once upon a time, when Peleus was hunting on Mount Pelion, a certain prince hid the sword of Peleus as he slept, and left him alone among the wild beasts. There he would have perished, for the Centaurs caught him; but old Cheiron the Centaur saved his life, and afterwards found his sword. For some time after that, he lived with Cheiron, and hunted the wild beasts.

There was a sea-nymph, named Thetis, who was so beautiful that two of the great gods fell in love with her. One was Poseidon, lord of the sea, who knew all the Nereids that lived in the coral caves under the waters; but he had never seen the equal of Thetis, and he wanted to make her his wife. The other god was Zeus himself. No doubt he had heard Poseidon talking about this young beauty, and went to have a look at her himself.

At all events, the brothers fell out about it; and as they could not agree, they asked the advice of the wise Themis, the goddess of justice and law. She said at once, "Before I give my opinion, I ought to tell you one thing: her son will be stronger than his father. I should advise you to let her marry a mortal man, and that will be better for both of you."

The gods were persuaded at once. "No stronger sons for me," said Zeus, "that is my view, whatever you may think of it, brother Poseidon." "I agree with that," said Poseidon. "Well, who shall be her husband?" Zeus answered. "She shall have a good one, and I know a man who has lately distinguished himself by honourable conduct, one Peleus, who is living at present with old Cheiron in his cave."

Then a message was sent to Peleus, telling him that Zeus was ready to give him a beautiful nymph of the sea, on condition that he must catch her first. Cheiron told him about it. He said, "Like the other creatures of the sea, she can change her shape. If you want her for a wife, you must catch her, and hold her fast."

Peleus felt sure he would win. Perhaps he had learnt something from his wrestling match with Atalanta; but at least he knew now that the gods were on his side. So he went down to the sea-shore with Cheiron; and there was Thetis, waiting for him; there were the nymphs of the sea, all looking on; and there were the gods, as pleased as possible to see a new kind of wrestling match.

Peleus caught hold of the two wrists of Thetis, and held fast. Thetis changed first into a tree, and he held fast to the two branches he found in his hands; that was easy enough. Next, she became an eagle, and he held her two wings. And then suddenly he found himself holding the strong paws of a tiger. Still he would not let go; and now he was holding a great lion. I suppose Thetis was losing her patience, for the next thing she did, was to change into wind. I do not know how he held the wind, but he did, and so he did when she changed into fire, which scorched him, and then water, which put out the fire. His hands were still clenched, when he saw that he held two of the long arms of a giant squid. But that was a mistake on the part of Thetis; for he held these arms so tight, that she could not change any more, and so she became at last Thetis.

Now Thetis knew that she was beaten, so she put a good face on the matter, and agreed to be married to Peleus. And it was indeed a magnificent wedding, which was remembered all through Greek history. There was a grand feast, there were visitors from far and near, and to cap all, there was a half-circle of noble thrones, and the gods themselves seated upon them, to share in the feasts, while the Muses sang and played on the flute and harp, and the Seasons danced in the midst. The Fates also sang, the Spinner, the Portioner, and Never-turn-back. They sang:

> "Fortunate pair! Your child shall be a boy
> Who shall lay low the enemy hosts at Troy.
> No other man shall be so brave and strong.
> Run on, my spindles, pull the thread along!"

Cheiron gave Peleus a great ashen spear, which we often hear of in the stories about him; Poseidon gave him two immortal horses, named Chestnut and Bay, and the other gods gave him weapons and armour.

Peleus had now got his wish, and a divine wife; but he found out, as many men have done, that it is better to marry one of your own rank in life. Thetis bore a son, Achillês, and she loved him very much, but she wanted to make him immortal, like herself. She dipped him in the awful river of Styx, to make his body safe against wounds; but she had to hold him by the heel and ankle, and so his heel was left unprotected, and it was a wound in the heel that killed him in the end. Not content with a water-bath, she used fire too. Every night she used to lay him in the fire, as Demeter did to another baby, if you remember; this was done to burn away all of him that was mortal, and in the day she used to anoint him with the gods' own ambrosia, which made them immortal. But one night Peleus caught her at it, and when she saw the child writhing amid the flames, he cried out. Then Thetis caught up the child, and threw him down on the ground, and fled away shrieking to the sea: into the sea she plunged, and returned to her father Nereus and the sea-nymphs her sisters, and came back no more. Peleus lived sad and deserted in his palace halls.

But he took the child Archillês, and gave him over to Cheiron to train him up. Cheiron fed him on the marrow of lions, to make him brave and strong, and on the marrow of stags, to make him swift of foot; he became so swift, that he could catch any animal by running after it, and he was always called by everyone Swiftfoot Achillês. When he grew older, Cheiron made him a little sword and a little spear and a little shield, and little bow and arrows, and sent him out to catch what he could. So he practised the arts of war on mice and moles, which he was to practise later in real battle. There we will leave him to grow up, while we turn to other things that were happening in the world.

XXXII. *Apollo and Admetos*

You remember how Zeus once had to prevent a rebellion among the gods, and how Apollo and Poseidon were punished by doing a year's hard labour on earth. Zeus had to punish Apollo again for another offence; and this time he had to be a man's servant again for a year. So he came down into Thessaly.

Admetos was king of Pherai, in Thessaly, and when he was engaging his servants for the year, he saw a noble young man waiting to offer himself. "Who are you?" he asked. "You are a stranger to me." "Yes, sir," said Apollo, for he it was, "I am a good hand with sheep and cattle, and I will serve you well." So he was engaged; and so well he did his work, that in the spring all the cows had twin calves, and all the ewes had twin lambs, and all the nanny-goats had twin kids, safe and sound. Admetos was very much pleased with his man, and made much of him.

Sometimes the young herdsman used to bring out a strange instrument, made of a tortoise-shell, with strings fixed across it; he used to touch the strings with his fingers, and bring out beautiful music that made them all want to dance. But sometimes the King met him early in the morning, and saw wreaths of flowers about his head; he would stand still to gaze at the rising sun, and seemed not to see Admetos at all. But strangest of all, when sacrifice was made to the gods, the stranger was never there.

Admetos was a great horseman, for the Thessalians loved horses; and once he went to the games at the court of King Pelias, whom you remember in the story of Jason. He won all his contests, but he lost his heart; for his eyes fell on Alcestis, the daughter of Pelias, and he fell in love with her at once. When he asked Pelias for his daughter, every one thought it would be a fine match for her with the rich Thessalian King; but Pelias, who was a proud man, smiled grimly and said, "It is no light honour to wed a maiden who has divine blood in her veins. One who wooes her must drive up to my door in a chariot drawn by a lion and a boar. If not, it is fated that she must die on her wedding day."

Admetos, also a proud man, said at once, "Fear nothing for that; you shall see the sight you ask for, without fail." But in his mind he did not think he could do it; so with all his prizes, he returned home downcast and gloomy.

As he walked in the evening, and thought what a fool he had been to make such a promise, he saw his young herdsman, and greeted him. Apollo said, "You seem to be unhappy, sir; what is it?" "I have been a fool," said Admetos. "I asked Pelias for his daughter, and he told me that I must come to fetch her, driving a lion and a wild boar." Apollo said, "I think I can help you, if you will let me go away for a few days." Admetos was glad to consent, for what else could he do? So he returned to his palace, and Apollo took his bow and arrows, and set off for the mountains.

The days were long while Admetos waited; but at last came a morning, when he opened his eyes to see the young herdsman standing by his bed, and he heard him call out, "Awake, King Admetos! Your team is ready." Then he arose, and came down to the door, and there stood an ivory chariot, with a lion and a boar under the yoke. "Farewell," said Apollo, "but be sure to return this evening, for at sunset the beasts will be wild again." Admetos leapt lightly into the chariot, and caught up the reins, and away.

How the people stared to see this new team go by! And when he came to the city of Pelias, what commotion there was in the streets, what amazement, to hear the padding of the lion's paws, and the clatter of the boar's hooves, and their growls as they ran through the streets! To the palace of Pelias they came, and drew up at the door. "Welcome!" said Pelias—"here is your bride! And you, my daughter, thank the man who has taken away your curse, and made you able to be a happy wife and mother. But you, sir, pray deign to stay this night with us, and let us hold a fast to do you honour."

"No," said Admetos, remembering what Apollo had told him; "I cannot delay: I must be gone at once." So he led Alcestis to the chariot, and they both mounted, and away drove Admetos with his bride. When they came to the sacred grove close by his own city, there stood the young herdsman. The beasts at once came to a stop, and would not move; so the pair dismounted, and left the team with him, and made the rest of their way on foot.

There was great joy when they arrived, although every one was surprised to see them walking. Sacrifices were made to the gods, and all made ready for the wedding. But in the excitement, Artemis was forgotten; there was no sacrifice for her, and the hard goddess never failed to punish that slight. So when Admetos opened the door of his bridal chamber, he saw a heap of snakes writhing on the floor. He understood this to be a sign of the anger of some deity.

Admetos again asked the help of Apollo; and Apollo succeeded in making Artemis friendly again. I do not know how he did it, but Artemis was his sister, and no doubt she knew that Apollo could do her many a good turn if he liked. She forgave Admetos, at all events; and Apollo persuaded the Fates to grant him a special favour: that when his time came to die, his life might be saved if some one else would die for him.

Soon after that, Apollo's year was up, and he returned to Olympos.

Time went on. Alcestis bore two children, Admetos was happy, his kingdom was prosperous: but a day came when he fell ill, and he knew that he was to die. He turned his face to the wall, and said nothing, for he did not wish to ask another to die for him.

Every one knew what the Fates had promised, but no

one came forward to offer his life for the king. Of course they all talked about it, and every one thought that every one else ought to die, but no one was anxious to be the man. "Why does not his old father die?" they said. "He has had his life; there is not much left to him anyhow." But the old man did not see it like that. "I am sorry for my son," he said. "Poor fellow! To die so young, and so happy. But I am quite happy too; life is sweet—why should one give it up before the gods call him? Let every man bear his own fate." Even the old Queen thought much the same. They were sorry for their son, but sorrier for themselves: and Admetos prepared to die.

But Alcestis said nothing at all. She came in the evening, and lay down by her husband's side; and in her heart she said, "I will die for my husband." So she went quietly to sleep, and in the morning she lay there dead.

Admetos awoke to find himself as strong and well as ever he was. He could not understand why, until he looked on his wife's face, and saw that she was dead. Then he understood that she had given her life for him. But life was too dear at such a price. He knew that his happiness was over, but there was no help for it; and Alcestis was prepared for burial, and carried out to the tomb.

Just at this moment, who should come up but Heraclês. Admetos was bound by the laws of hospitality to entertain a guest; so Heraclês was led apart from the signs of mourning, and the servants provided him with all he needed. After his dinner, he asked where Admetos was. Some excuse was made, but at last he began to suspect something. "Why do you look so gloomy, man?" he said: and by degrees the story came out.

Then Heraclês was angry. "He should not have let me feast," said he, "with mourning in the house, and especially with his own wife dead. But it was a noble hospitality, after all! Perhaps I can do something to repay it." Then a thought came into his mind. "Where is the tomb?" he asked. "Let me go and pay my respects to the queen." They showed him, and he entered the tomb.

He was there a long time, and there were sounds of a struggle, which disturbed the servants, but they did not like to go in. For King Hadês himself was within that place, and Heraclês wrestled with King Hadês, until he consented to let Alcestis come back to life. So Heraclês raised up Alcestis from her bier, and led her, veiled, to the palace; and there, to the amazement of the world, he gave back Alcestis to her husband safe and sound.

XXXIII. *Helios and Phaëthon*

When Apollo used to gaze at the sun, at the time he was herdsman to Admetos, I think he was making a plan already to take it over himself; for you know he was an ambitious young god. But so far the sun was in charge of Helios, one of the old Titans, and a nephew of Cronos. Zeus left him alone, because he did his job all right, and never wanted to rebel.

But Helios had a boy of his own, a young fellow named Phaëthon, or the Shiner: and Phaëthon was as ambitious as Apollo.

He often watched his father driving the horses of the sun: so easily he did it, that Phaëthon thought he could do the same. But he did not dare to say so plainly; he made a roundabout plan to get what he wanted.

So one evening, when Helios sat down to rest, Phaëthon said to him, "Father, am I really your son? You are so magnificent that I feel very small beside you."

Helios answered, "Indeed you are my son: and to prove it, I will grant you anything you may choose to ask."

Phaëthon said, "I thank you, my father! And I will prove that I am your son indeed! Let me drive your horses for one day!"

Then Helios struck his forehead with his hand; he saw what a fool he had been to make such a promise. But the promise was made, and even the gods cannot recall their gifts. He said, at last:

"Ah, that was a rash promise. That is the only thing I would deny you, my boy. You are mortal, and no mortal can do that task. Indeed, even Zeus himself could not do it; he can manage a thunderbolt, but he cannot drive the horses of the Sun. Let me persuade you to choose something else. Think now, while I tell you how difficult is the task. The first part of the way is a steep ascent, and the

horses find it all they can do to climb up. Then you are in
high heaven, and to look down on the sea and the earth
makes even me dizzy. And last there is a steep way down-
wards, which needs all my strength and skill to hold the
horses back. Every evening the goddess of the sea trembles
with fear that I may fall headlong, and make the waters
boil. And think of the dangers of the way! All the while,
the heavens are whirling around at a great rate, and you
may easily dash the chariot against the north or south
pole. And there are strange monsters on all sides: a wild
Bull, thrusting his horns at you; an Archer, shooting his
arrows; a Scorpion, with a sharp sting; and a Crab, sweep-
ing his great claws all around. And the horses are breathing
out flame from their mouths and nostrils the whole time."

But Phaëthon would not listen; indeed, all this made
him more eager to try.

So next morning, when Eos opened the gates of the
dawn, and all the stars were driven away, and the moon
faded, Helios led Phaëthon to his car, and commanded
the Seasons to put his horses to the yoke. Phaëthon gazed
in wonder at the car: its wheels were of gold, and silver
spokes, and jewels flashed from the fittings. Still more did
he wonder at the horses, as they pranced out breathing
fire. Helios with a sad heart anointed his son's face with
sacred ointment, to protect him from the fire, and placed
on his head his own crown with its golden spikes. Then he
said:

"Be careful, my son, and spare the lash. Look for the
tracks of my wheels; for the course is not straight through
the heavens, but it goes slantwise, in a wide curve which
keeps clear of both north pole and south pole alike. Now
take the reins, unless you will be well advised at the last
moment, and choose another gift."

"No, my father," said Phaëthon, "I fear nothing; I will
show that I am your son!" And he mounted the car, and
took the reins.

The four horses, Fiery, Shiny, Scorcher and Blazer,
snorted and champed; and at once they felt the light weight
of the boy, and his unskilful hands. They took the bit be-
tween their teeth, and leapt up, tossing the chariot about,
and dashed straight up the sky. They did not keep to the
proper path, but went straight for the Bear, who had never

been so hot before in his life. Phaëthon looked down and his head swam; he looked back, but that way he could not go; he looked forward to the west, and how far off that seemed! He saw the Crab, waving his claws, and he saw the Scorpion with the great sting in his tail—a panic seized him, and he dropped the reins. When the horses felt the reins on their backs, they just ran away.

Then the earth began to feel it: the forests caught fire, Athos was in a blaze, Caucasos and Ida melted their snows, and all the people of Africa were burnt black, as they have been ever since. Phaëthon choked with the flames about him. But Zeus had pity on the world. He sent a thunderbolt and struck Phaëthon; down fell the chariot into the sea; and down fell Phaëthon into the river Eridanos. The horses went at top speed to the west, and there they were rubbed down, and put in the golden boat to carry them back to the east.

Phaëthon's sisters wept and lamented his death; they wept and would not be comforted, as they stood by their brother's tomb. Indeed, they stood there weeping so long that gradually they felt themselves growing into the soil. Bark grew up around them, from the feet upwards, and they became poplar trees. But their tears continued to flow, and as they flowed, the tears became drops of amber.

Helios was full of sorrow, and said, "I have had enough of this task; anyone may drive the horses of the Sun for me. Let me rest." But Zeus would not allow it. He provided a new chariot, and commanded Helios to drive as before, and so he did, until at a later time, Apollo turned him out, and took over the Sun himself.

PART 5

XXXIV. *Orpheus and Eurydicê*

Orpheus was one of the heroes who went in quest of the Golden Fleece. I did not tell you then all the things he did, because there were so many other things to tell; but I will tell you some now. To the sound of his harp, the ship Argo glided down into the sea. The sound of his harp made the Clashing Rocks stand still just one minute, when the Argo was passing through. The sound of his harp helped to send the sleepless dragon to sleep.

You see he was a rare hand with the harp; and no wonder, for his father was Apollo, and Apollo taught him to play upon his own harp. He played so beautifully, that all the wild beasts on Mount Olympos used to come and lie down all around him, to listen. More than that, even the trees would pluck up their roots, if they were not too old and too deep, and hop along to listen. Even the rocks rolled out of their places, and came to listen. All the country people were enchanted; the wild Satyrs used to dance around him, wagging their tails.

He married a wife named Eurydicê, whom he loved very much. One day Eurydicê trod on a snake, which bit her foot, and she died.

Orpheus would not be comforted. He played on his harp no more; he wandered over the mountains, and through the forests, and mourned his lost wife. At last he determined that he would go down to the dark house of Hadês, and bring her back.

So he entered the dark cave, and traversed the dark tunnel which led through the earth, to the dark house of Hadês. When he came to the gate, the three-headed dog Cerberos growled, and would have bitten him; but Orpheus played a

142

soft tune on his harp, and the dog dropped his three heads on his paws, and gently wagged his tail, and let Orpheus go by.

When he came to the great hall of Hadês, what a sight met his eyes! There sat King Hadês and Queen Persephonê, on their thrones. There sat the three Judges of the Dead, Minos, Rhadamanthys and Aiacos—for there is justice in the house of Hadês. Every soul, when it comes into that place, must give account for deeds done in the body: those who are good are dismissed to the Elysian Fields, to be at peace; those who are bad receive punishment proper to their deeds.

There Orpheus saw some of the great sinners enduring their punishment. He saw a family of nine-and-forty sisters, the Danaïds, who had all been married on one day, and had murdered their husbands in the night. They were condemned to draw water, and carry it in jars to a huge vessel with holes in the bottom, so as fast as they poured the water in, it ran out.

He saw the punishment of the cruel King Tantalos. In his life on earth, Tantalos once entertained the gods at a feast. Like the wicked King of Arcadia, he wanted to see if they really had more wisdom than men. So he killed his own son Pelops, and cooked the body, and offered it to the gods to eat. They all knew it at once, and refused, except Demeter, who ate a bit of the shoulder, because she had just lost her daughter and did not know what she was doing. Pelops was brought back to life, and made well again, all but the bit of his shoulder, which was a-missing: but Demeter put an ivory shoulder in its place. This Tantalos was punished by being hungry and thirsty for ever. He stood in the middle of a lake of water: when he bent down his head to drink, the water all slid away; if he scooped up a handful, the water ran through his fingers. All round the water grew trees laden with fruit, apples and pears, figs, and grapes, and oranges; when he stretched out his hand to pluck one, the tree whisked it away into the air above him. Did your father ever call you a tantalizing brat? If so, he was reminding you of Tantalos, who was always disappointed when he hoped for something good.

He saw Sisyphos, the most cunning and deceitful of men, who had betrayed the secrets of the gods. His punishment

was to roll a huge stone up to the top of a hill: he pushed
with head and shoulders, panting and sweating and cov-
ered with dust; but whenever he got to the top, the stone
would gently slide off on one side or the other, and roll
down to the bottom. Then he had to begin all over again.

He saw Ixion, who also had committed an act of treach-
ery to the gods. His punishment was the strangest of all. He
was fastened to a wheel with four spokes, one for each leg
and arm, and the wheel went round and round for ever.

That was the scene which met the eye of Orpheus, as
he entered the dark house of Hadês. The soul of Eurydicê
was there waiting, for her case had not yet been heard;
there were so many waiting for judgement. But Orpheus
pleaded with Hadês, that he might take her back to life.

Hadês said, "Why should I treat her otherwise than I
treat the other souls?"

Orpheus was silent: then his eyes flashed, and he said, in
a loud voice, "This is why!" and struck up a tune on his
harp. The melody began soft, then rose, and rang loudly
through the dark hall: and as the melody sounded, Hadês
leaned forward on his throne and listened, Persephonê
turned her head and sat still and listened, the three judges
ceased their questions and listened, the Danaïds stood still
and listened, and let the water do what it would, the water
ceased to run out of the holes, Tantalos's lake stood still
and Tantalos had a good drink, then he listened too, the
stone of Sisyphos rolled up to Orpheus and lay still, Ixion's
wheel stood still and Ixion with it, to listen to the wonder-
ful sounds. At last Hadês said: "Your music is worth a
life. Take her and go: but be very careful never to look
back at her till you come to your own door."

Orpheus was glad enough to have her on any conditions;
so he turned round, and went towards the gate, still playing
upon his harp, and Eurydicê followed him. Out of the gate
he went, still playing, past the three-headed Cerberos, along
the dark tunnel, out of the dark cave, and then he thought
to himself, "I wonder if Eurydicê is following," for he could
not hear her footsteps. Without thinking, he turned to look:
there she was, close behind—but even as he looked, she
uttered a cry, she began to fade, and in a few moments,
like a wisp of smoke, she had vanished.

Now there was no hope for Orpheus. But he seems to

have learnt the wisdom of the gods by his journey to the house of Hadês; for he no longer played on his harp, but he made wonderful poems, telling mankind what to do if they wished to please the gods, and to be happy after death. Some say he also taught them to eat only vegetables, and not to kill animals for food. Perhaps he remembered how sensible the animals were in listening to his music; but that can hardly be the reason, for the trees listened too, and no doubt the vegetables would have listened if they had been handy.

But Orpheus would not marry another wife. There were a number of wild women in Thrace, where he lived, and they used to hold feasts in honour of Dionysos every year, and madden themselves with wine. Some say they were angry because Orpheus would not take one of them to wife: whatever the reason may be, these women set on him and killed him, and cut off his head, and threw it into the river Hebros. The river carried it into the sea, and it floated across to the island of Lesbos, by the town of Methymna, where it was washed ashore. And ever since that time, right down to our own day, the nightingales in the olive trees round Methymna sing more sweetly than any other nightingales in the world.

XXXV. *Danaê and the Shower of Gold*

You remember the Danaïds in the dark house of Hadês, who had to fill up a huge vessel with holes in the bottom. Their father was Danaos, who had fifty daughters, but his brother Aigyptos (or Egypt) had fifty sons. Danaos was afraid that the fifty sons were going to kill him. He agreed that they should be married to his fifty daughters, and then he gave each of the daughters a dagger, and told them to kill their husbands as soon as they fell asleep. Forty-nine of them did so, but the fiftieth did not, and I think I may tell you her name, as I have spared you the names of the other nine-and-forty. It was Hypermnestra. She did not kill her husband, and after many years we come now to the story of her grandsons, Acrisios and his brother Proitos.

That is a long rigmarole, to be sure, but we have come to the point at last.

Acrisios and his twin brother Proitos were always fighting together, as brothers often do; and when they grew up, Acrisios drove his brother out, and remained King of Argos by himself. But an oracle foretold that he was to be killed by his grandson, if there should be one. He had a daughter Danaê, and he determined to make sure that she should never have a son: so he built a strong tower of brass, and shut her up in the tower, along with her waiting-women, and allowed no one else to go in.

This was a cruel fate, and Danaê was very unhappy; but what could she do? She could see from her tower all the people going about their business, and enjoying their life: feasts and processions, weddings and dances, and there she was, left all alone, and bored to death. No one dared to come in, and the attendants and guards were too much afraid of the King to allow anyone to visit her.

But Zeus, who sees all things, saw Danaê in her tower; and as she was beautiful, Zeus fell in love with her, and resolved to make her his wife. It was easy enough for him, but he did not march up to the door, and demand admittance; he made another plan, quite a new one.

So it happened that one day, as Danaê sat melancholy in her chamber at the top of the tower, she saw the air become thick with a kind of mist. Soon the mist grew into soft flakes of gold, like a golden snow, and fell all over the room. Then the flakes gathered up into a solid shape; and she saw standing before her what she thought was a noble young man, and his body was covered with bright clothing that shone like gold.

"Who are you?" said Danaê, astonished.

"Do not fear me," said he, "for I have heard of your sad fate, and I have come to comfort you, if you will be my lover."

Danaê was delighted to have so noble a lover, when she expected none at all, not even an ugly one. So after that, Zeus would often come and visit her in a shower of golden snow-flakes, unknown to all, and after his visit, he would melt into golden snowflakes again, and pass away on the wind.

Acrisios knew nothing of all this; and what was his

amazement, one day, when a messenger came panting before him, and said:

"Sir, your daughter has borne a son!"

"What!" said he. "Did I not forbid you to let anyone go in?"

"Sir," he answered, "we have let no one go in, we know nothing about it! Do not blame us, we have done our duty, I swear it."

Then Acrisios was angry and frightened at once. Whatever the cause, there was his grandson, and the oracle said he was to kill Acrisios one day. Acrisios did not like to murder his daughter and the baby outright; but he quieted his conscience by saying they should have a chance. So he put both of them into a large chest or hutch, and fastened the cover on it, with holes to let in the air; and then he set them adrift on the sea.

The winds blew, and the waves rose, and the foam drenched the mother and her son, as they lay in the chest. The tears ran down her cheeks, and she threw her arms about the boy and said, "Ah, my baby, what sorrow is yours! And yet you weep not. You sleep quiet like a suckling babe, in this dark chest: you care not for the salt foam on your hair, nor for the whistling wind, as you lie in your purple wrappings, with your soft cheek against mine. If you knew your danger, you would open your little ear to my words. Sleep on, my babe, and may the sea sleep, and may Zeus your father send us help!"

XXXVI. *Perseus and the Gorgon Medusa*

Zeus heard the mother's prayer; the chest was washed up on the shore of a little island named Seriphos. A man of the island came along, and saw the chest, which was richly carved, and he thought it a great find. But when he prized off the lid, what was his surprise to see Danaê and the baby inside! He was a kind man, and took them in, and they lived in his house while the boy grew up.

The boy's name was Perseus; and he grew up to be strong, and brave, and handsome, and won prizes in the athletic games of the island. So he was noticed by the King,

Polydectês; and before long the King caught sight of his mother, Danaê, and determined to make her his wife.

But Danaê would not hear of it: she, the wife of the immortal Zeus, to give herself to the petty chief of a small island! The King persecuted her, but he was afraid of Perseus; and he soon saw that Perseus must be got out of the way.

Accordingly, he pretended to flatter him on his success in the games. "You are a fine boy," he said. "You can beat every one in this island at running and boxing and wrestling. In fact, you are wasted in a small place like this. You ought to try some great task, and make a name in the world, like the real heroes." You see, he did not know that Perseus was a real hero, as being a son of Zeus; Danaê kept that secret to herself.

"What do you mean, sir?" asked Perseus. "Just tell me something worth trying for!"

"I will," said the King. "Go and bring me Medusa's head."

Perseus asked, "Who is Medusa?"

The King said, "There are three awful sisters, the three Gorgons, named the Strong, the Leaper, and the Queen, that is Medusa. Strong and Leaper are ugly things, but the Gorgon Medusa is the most beautiful creature in the world. I want her head, never mind why."

"Where can they be found?" asked Perseus.

The King said, "Far away in the west, in the land of darkness. You must find your own way, for I do not know any more about it."

This fired the ambition of Perseus, and he determined to fetch Medusa's head.

The gods knew all this, of course; and as Perseus was thinking what to do, suddenly Athena appeared to him, and said:

"Perseus, do you know me?"

"Indeed I do!" said Perseus. "You are the great goddess Athena."

"Well," said Athena, "we gods are going to help you. First of all look at this," and she showed him the image of a head: the face was very beautiful, but cruel and cold and unhappy, and instead of hair, it had curling ringlets of snakes all round. "That is the Gorgon Medusa," she said, "but if you look at the real face, you will be turned into stone."

"Then how can I get the head?" said Perseus.

"Take this shield," and she gave him a shield, smooth and shining, like a mirror, "and when you come to Medusa, keep your back to her, and see her image in the shield, so as to strike back over your shoulder. Then cut off her head, and put it in this bag," and she gave him a large bag of leather. "Be careful to leave her sisters alone, for they are immortal; Medusa alone is mortal, and she can be killed."

"But how shall I find the way?" he asked.

"Wait a minute," said Athena, and then all of a sudden, there were Hermês and Hadês, who appeared out of nothing, as the gods can do. But Hermês said, "See here, I lend you my winged shoes: put them on your feet, and you will fly through the air like a bird. And here is a sharp sickle, to cut off Medusa's head." Then Hadês said, "And I lend you my cap of darkness; when you have it on, you will be invisible, and no one will see you."

"And now," said Athena, "you must fly away to the west, until you come to the Three Old Hags, who alone know the way to the Gorgons. They have only one eye between them, and one tooth, which they lend about as they want them. Their names are the Buzzer, the Terror, and the Fury, and they keep watch over their sisters, the Gorgons. They live in the west, beyond the sun and moon, and you will have to persuade them to tell you the way."

This did not sound hopeful, but there was no more to be done, as the three gods had all disappeared.

So Perseus slung the shield and the sickle about his shoulders, and hung the bag over his back, and put on the cap of darkness, and fastened the winged shoes to his feet: then he rose in the air.

On and on he flew, over land and sea, over mountain and forest, beyond the sun and the moon into the dark regions of the west. No doubt the winged shoes guided him, for he came straight to the place where the Three Old Hags had their dwelling.

Terror said, "I hear a noise in the air: what is it?"

Fury said, "Give me the tooth, and let me bite it!" So

the tooth was passed to Fury, but she could see nothing, because the eye was in the socket of Buzzer.

Terror said, "Sister, what can you see?"

Buzzer said, "I can see nothing at all, but I hear a shivering in the air." For the cap of darkness made Perseus invisible.

"Pass me the eye!" said Fury. "You are as blind as a bat!" She put the eye into her own socket, but saw nothing. Then Terror said, "Pass it here, will you!"

But as Fury took out the eye, and held it towards her sister, Perseus neatly swooped in between them and caught it. "Now then," said Fury, "can *you* see anything?" for she thought Terror had taken it, and of course the eye could see nothing as it passed between them, with no socket to sit in.

"Give me the eye!" said Terror.

"I have given it," said Fury, "and I felt you take it!"

"I did not!" said Terror.

"Here," said Fury, "take the tooth, and give her a nip," but as she held out the tooth, Perseus swooped down quickly and caught it. Then there was a frightful quarrel, as each Old Hag thought the others were playing a trick on her. In the midst of it, Perseus called out:

"Fear nothing, mighty beings, the eye and the tooth are safe: I hold them in my hand."

There was a sudden silence. Then they all cried out at once, "Who is that?"

He replied, "I am Perseus, and I come to ask you the way to the place where the Gorgons are."

"We will not tell you!" they all cried out.

"Then I will not give you back the eye and the tooth. Good-bye," and he made as if to go.

"Wait, wait, wait!" they cried. They did their best to persuade Perseus to give back the eye and the tooth, but he was firm, and in the end, they had to tell him the way to go. Then he flew off, saying, "When I come back, you shall have your eye and your tooth safe and sound."

Thus the Three Old Hags could not defend their sisters, the Gorgons, and Perseus came to the place where they were.

He found the Gorgons asleep. Two of them had golden wings and bronze claws, and enormous teeth, and they would have made short work of Perseus if they had caught him. But he was careful to be quiet; and approaching Medusa backwards, he looked at her image in the bright shield, and struck a blow behind him, and killed her. Then he cut off the head, and put it into his bag. Drops of blood fell from the neck: and from them sprang up Pegasos, the winged horse, who flew away to the stables of Zeus. The two sisters awoke, and tried to catch Perseus in their claws; but he was too quick for them. He flew back to the Three Old Hags, and gave them the eye in turn and let them have a look at him when he took off his cap. He gave back the tooth too, but he took care to give it just as he was about to fly away, and he gave it to one who had not the eye at that moment.

XXXVII. *Perseus and Andromeda*

The journey back was more of a roundabout. No doubt Perseus thought he would never have a better chance of seeing the world. He seems to have flown over Africa and Asia, and he even visited the people who live behind the North Wind. These were a very happy people, who had a kind of earthly paradise, almost as good as the Islands of the Blest, where all the great heroes went, and lived for ever at peace.

As he passed over Africa, he saw a huge figure with its head in the clouds, and when he looked close, it was old Atlas the Titan, holding up the heavens upon his shoulder.

Old Atlas hailed him, and said, "Stranger, you must be the hero Perseus, who according to the oracle will set me free. Show me the Gorgon's head!" He was weary of holding up the heavens, and he thought with pleasure of the short holiday he had, when Heraclês paid him a visit.

Perseus took the head out of his bag, and held it out towards Atlas, but he was careful to turn his own head away. Then he put it back in the bag; and when he looked at Atlas, he saw that his body had changed into a great rock, his hair and beard into forests. So Atlas rested at last from his long labour. If you look on the map, there

you will see the Atlas Mountains still, and they hold up
the heavens quite as well as the old Titan did.

As Perseus came nearer home, on a bright sunny day,
he looked down: and there on the coast of Palestine, near
the port of Joppa, which you have read of in the Bible,
he saw a long procession of people moving towards the sea.
They were leading a beautiful maiden, and soon they bound
her fast with chains to a rock and went away weeping and
wailing loud.

This maiden was named Andromeda, and she was
daughter to the King of that place. Her mother was a vain
and foolish woman, and she had boasted that her daughter
was more beautiful than all the nymphs of the sea. Accord-
ingly the god of the sea, Poseidon, the father of these
nymphs, was very angry, and he flooded the coast, and
sent a sea-monster to devour anyone he could catch. At
last, after many prayers, he consented to spare the people,
if the King would give his daughter for the sea-monster to
devour; and that was why they left her chained to a rock,
and went away.

Perseus did not know this. He only saw the maiden
chained to a rock, and an ugly monster swimming in from
the sea. The maiden gazed at the monster with staring eyes,
full of horror; the monster lashed the sea with his tail, and
his green sides shone in the sunlight with scales of hard
horn, his mouth opened and showed a red throat and sharp
rows of teeth. Neither of them looked up, to see a new
kind of bird swoop down from the sky. Down came Perseus,
like an eagle, holding the sickle of Hermês which had cut
off the Gorgon's head. He attacked the monster from be-
hind, and gave him a deep cut on the neck. Then there was
a terrible fight, but the monster could not reach Perseus,
and Perseus flew in and out like an eagle, cutting under the
monster's scales, until at last he cut its throat, and the body
fell back lifeless upon the sea.

You may imagine how glad Andromeda was, and how
Perseus loosed her chains, and led her back to her father;
and how glad her father was, and how willingly he con-
sented when Perseus asked him that Andromeda might be
his wife. Had he not well earned the prize?

There was only one difficulty: that the King had promised her to some one else. This was a man named Phineus, who came up in a rage, and said, "Where is my bride?"

Perseus said, "Where were you, when the sea-monster was going to devour your bride?"

Phineus said, "I could not help her; why should I be swallowed too?"

Perseus said, "If you did not care enough for your bride to strike a blow for her life, you have no claim now."

Phineus said, "We will see about that. Here, you men!" and he called to his bodyguard, who stood under arms, with threatening looks. But Perseus did not wait for more. He took out the Gorgon's head from his bag, and showed it to them: and there they stood, turned into stone.

Then there was a grand wedding, and high rejoicings. But Perseus had to leave his bride there for the time being, because he must go back to Seriphos, and hand over the Gorgon's head to Polydectês. So he flew to Seriphos.

When he came to Seriphos, he put off his winged shoes, and walked to the town. But he could not find his mother. The fact was, King Polydectês had persecuted her, and told her she must be his wife, whether she liked it or not. He knew only that Perseus had gone, but he did not know how, and he felt sure he would never come back. Then Perseus found his mother in the temple, where she had fled for refuge, and with her the kind man who had brought him up, who was the King's brother.

When Danaê saw Perseus, she cried, "Oh my son! You have come back, and I thought you were dead!"

"What are you doing here?" he asked.

She said, "The King was so violent and threatening, that I have fled to this temple for refuge. But I am afraid even here, for he says he will come and fetch me out. And there he is!"

Indeed, there he was, with his bodyguard of soldiers, come to drag Danaê from the temple.

"Come out!" he cried. "My patience is at an end.—But who is this? Never Perseus, returned from his journey? Welcome, dear boy!" for he began to be afraid now.

Then Perseus said, "Do not call me dear boy, when you want to lay violent hands on my mother."

"Nonsense," he answered; "but tell me about your journey. Did you get the Gorgon's head?"

"Oh yes," said Perseus, "would you like to see it?"

"Indeed I should," said the King.

Then Perseus whispered to his mother, "Turn your head away," and as she turned away, he drew out the Gorgon's head from the bag, and turned it towards Polydectês.

As Polydectês looked at it, a shiver ran through him, and in a moment he was a statue of stone, with the smile still on his false lips. His men also turned into stone, as many as looked upon the Gorgon's head, but those who were behind turned and ran out of the temple.

Perseus put the head back, and led his mother to her home. The kind man who had helped them became King, and all was well.

The three deities appeared once more to Perseus. Athena said, "I see you have got the head of Medusa, and come back safe. I am very glad to see it, and now you must return to us what we lent you."

Perseus thanked them all for their help. Then he gave the bag and the shield to Athena, and the cap to Hadês, and to Hermês the sickle and winged shoes; but the head of Medusa he gave to Athena, and Athena fixed it upon her shield. Ever after she bore the shield with the Gorgon's head; and if she showed it to her enemies, they turned into stone.

Perseus sent for his bride, and they lived a happy life. I need not tell you all that happened to him, but I have one thing more to tell.

There used to be games in the island of Seriphos, as you know; and once Acrisios came to attend them. Perseus had to throw a quoit in the games, and it went a little to one side, where Acrisios was craning his head forward to look on. The quoit caught his head, and killed him; and so the prophecy was fulfilled, which had made him so cruel to Danaê. This was quite an accident, for Perseus had been very kind to Acrisios; he even restored him to the throne when an enemy had turned him out.

XXXVIII. *Pegasos and Bellerophon*

You have heard how Pegasos, the winged horse, sprang up from the drops of blood that fell from the neck of Medusa. But why should a horse spring up from Medusa's blood? Because Medusa was the daughter of Phorcys, the old god of the sea, brother of old Mother Earth. When Zeus and his family came into power, the ancient deities were put out of power. The sea was taken by Poseidon, but old Phorcys lived there still in the depths.

Now the sea is full of horses, as I told you before. If you look over the sea when there is a fresh breeze, you will behold the horses of the sea, with their white manes, leaping to the top of the waves, and sinking again. Poseidon gave the horse to mankind; and so this winged horse, Pegasos, sprang up from the blood of Medusa, daughter of old Phorcys.

He was a beauty, the noblest horse man ever saw, a glossy bay colour, and besides his fours legs, he had wings on the shoulders. When he was made, he shook off the water from his wings and mane, and neighed loudly, and flew up to the house of Olympos. There Zeus kept him in the immortal stables; and he used to fly to earth and get the thunderbolts from the Cyclôpês, and bring them to Zeus when he wanted a new stock.

Once when he came to earth, he stamped on the rock with one foot, and a fountain of clear water gushed out, which ever afterwards flowed in plenty. This was on the rock of Corinth, and the fountain was called after him the Horse's Fountain, or Hippocrênê.

I will leave Pegasos a while in the immortal stables of Zeus, and you will soon see why I have told you about him. for I have now to tell you the story of another hero, named Bellerophon. Do you remember Sisyphos, who had to roll the stone up the hill in the dark house of Hadês? Bellerophon was his grandson.

Bellerophon was an unlucky man. He happened by accident to kill another man; and therefore he was obliged to run away from Corinth, where his father was King, and take refuge in another country. He found refuge with a King named Proitos. This King had also been unlucky; for he was the brother of Acrisios, whom you remember in the story of Danaê, the brother that he was always fighting with. Acrisios turned him out, and he took refuge with King Iobatês in Lycia. He married the daughter of Iobatês, and Iobatês helped him to make head against Acrisios, so that at last he had a kingdom of his own close by. Acrisios was King of Argos, and Proitos King of Tiryns. You have head all these names before, so they ought not to puzzle you very much.

As I said, the unlucky Bellerophon took refuge with the unlucky Proitos, who had become lucky again, and Bellerophon hoped that he might become lucky too: and so he was, for a good long time, and he became a great man at last.

But now his bad luck had a turn. For the King's wife was a bad wife; and when she saw Bellerophon every day, doing brave deeds, and as handsome as a god, she fell in love with him. Worse than that, she did not keep it to herself, but prayed Bellerophon to betray her husband, and to carry her off somewhere away from him. Bellerophon was ashamed to hear such a proposal, and would have nothing to do with it. Then the wife did the worst thing of all: for she complained to her husband that Bellerophon had insulted her. In fact, she told her husband that Bellerophon had done the very thing she had done herself, and wrongfully accused an innocent man.

Proitos believed his wife. It is hard for a man to think that his wife is a liar and a traitor, and it was natural that Proitos should take the word of his wife as true. But he was afraid to do anything openly against Bellerophon, because all the people admired him; and he made a cunning plan to destroy him. He wrote a letter to Iobatês.

You remember how Cadmos taught the alphabet to the Greeks; he brought it from Asia with him, and Iobatês, who lived in Asia, knew it too. No doubt he had taught Proitos his ABC's when he lived in his court; and Proitos wrote a letter in these strange signs, which nobody knew but himself, to Iobatês, and this was the letter: "Kill the bearer of this as soon as you can." Then he folded up the tablets, on which the message was written, and gave the letter to Bellerophon as an introduction to King Iobatês. "For," he said, "I have something I wish you to do, and Iobatês will tell you about it when you get there." Then Bellerophon took his leave, and departed, and the queen looked on, gloating over her coming revenge.

Bellerophon arrived safely at the court of King Iobatês, and the King received him with rich hospitality, as was the way of men in those days.

But as Bellerophon entered the hall of feasting, he had a great shock. For amongst those who stood round the King, he saw the wicked Queen, the wife of Proitos.

Or at least so he thought. The Queen was a most beautiful woman, and this woman was exactly like her, in figure, in colouring, and hair: but when he examined closer, she had a very different look on her face. The Queen was bold, she was modest, the Queen was hard, she was gentle: in fact, she looked as good as she was beautiful. In a moment, Bellerophon fell in love with the beautiful girl, and she with him.

"This," the King said, "is my daughter"—and so the two really were sisters, and that was why they were so much alike.

After the feasting was over, the King asked his errand. Bellerophon said, "Sir, King Proitos has sent a letter by me, written in strange signs which he said you would understand," and he presented the tablets which he had brought. The King took them, and put them aside until he had time to puzzle them out, for he did not read as easily as you or I do. I daresay he had never had a letter before.

When in the evening he did read the letter, he was horrified to find that all it said was, "Kill the bearer of this as soon as you can." If you are surprised that Proitos could ask such a thing without any reason, you must know that once Proitos had saved the life of Iobatês; and then Iobatês had promised, under oath, that he would do whatever Proitos might ask, if he were ever in need. So he was in perplexity: either he must break his oath, which was a terrible crime, or he must kill a man without any reason, and perhaps an innocent man. It was like the oath of Herod, which he kept by cutting off the head of John the Baptist. Of course you know that it was wrong to make such an oath, and therefore it was right not to keep it; but this King did not understand that.

But what was he to do? At last a way occurred to him, by which he thought he might keep his oath, and yet not hurt his conscience. You must wait a minute before I tell you what this way was.

For a long time past the country had been ravaged by a hideous monster called the Chimaira. The word means a Goat, but we have borrowed it in English in the form "chimera," to signify a tale of nonsense. But this was no tale of nonsense to the people whose cattle and sheep were carried off, or killed by its fiery breath, and their crops set in a blaze by a puff from its mouth. They said it was a huge monster, with a lion's head, and a goat's body, and a long snake instead of a tail. It left a horrible stench behind it, and all the land was laid waste, and the people ruined, or even killed.

Now then, the King thought, that if he sent Bellerophon to destroy this monster, he would be sure to be killed, and thus he might keep his oath without wrong. For it was a worthy enterprise to attack a monster like that, such a thing as Heraclês and Theseus were glad to do.

Accordingly, next day he said to Bellerophon, "King Proitos tells me how brave a warrior you are, and how you have fought for him. Will you do something for me?"

"Yes, if I can," said Bellerophon.

Then King Iobatês told him about the Chimaira and what havoc had been made in the country-side; and Bellerophon was sorry for the country people, and so he said, without really thinking about it, "I will destroy this monster."

"And if you do," said Iobatês, "I will give you my daughter to wife, if you wish it."

Imagine whether Bellerophon wished it! That was the one thing he did wish; and it made him all the more eager to destroy the monster.

Bellerophon went about the country, to ask what the monster was like. He saw burnt houses and burnt crops, and dead bodies lying about, and at last he found a countryman, crawling along, and looking more dead than alive. He said:

"My good man, can you tell me about this monster?"

"Ah, sir," he said, "it is an awful tale! There was a meeting, all the neighbours came in to a wedding, and they sang and danced and made merry. I was working on the farm not far off. Suddenly I heard a harsh sound in the air, like a corncrake, but very loud, like a dry rattle, very loud, and the sky looked a sort of green colour, full of smoky mist. They were all singing happily, when I heard a shriek, and saw a great ugly shape come down amongst them. They scattered this way and that, all shrieking now, until in a short time all was silent. I hid until it seemed to have gone away, and then I escaped."

"What was it like?" asked Bellerophon.

"Well," said the man, "I can hardly tell, I was so frightened. But it looked as big as a mountain! Like a lion too, and a snake whipping about it, but I was too much frightened to see clear."

This was the monster he had to fight. He did not know what to do, so he prayed to the gods for help.

That night he had a dream. A figure appeared to him, and said, "You must return to Corinth, and bring back the winged horse, Pegasos. For Pegasos often comes down from heaven to drink of the sweet water of the Horse's Fountain, which he made by a blow of his foot."

Bellerophon took this to be an answer to his prayer, as indeed it was; so he prepared to set out. He had to go in disguise, for you remember he was a banished man; and he went alone, that no one might guess who he was.

In due time he arrived in Corinth, and for many nights he watched at the Horse's Fountain, and saw nothing. But at last he saw the winged horse sailing through the sky, and shining in the moonlight. Down it came to the fountain, and drank. In a moment Bellerophon's hand was upon it, clutching at the mane; but the horse Pegasos shook him off with a flap of his wings, and soared away into the sky.

Indeed, it was foolish to think that he could catch an immortal horse as easily as all that. Bellerophon saw that it was foolish, and very sad he was, as he lay down to sleep in Athena's temple, with his head upon the altar steps.

But in the middle of the night, he was awakened, to see a great light in the temple; the light shone from the figure of the goddess Athena herself, who stood before him in full armour, holding something in her hand. She said, smiling,

"Are you asleep, Bellerophon? So you could not catch Pegasos?"

"No, my Queen," he said, "it was foolish to expect it."

"But not foolish if I help you," she said. "See here: this is a charm for horses, a golden master for mouth and mind. Take it, and when you have succeeded, give thanks to the Lord of the Allmastering Sea, your father's father."

What she gave him was a twisted bar of gold, with two long streamers, running from each end, and a curved golden ribbon rounded over the top. He could not make it out. He had never seen anything like it before, but he resolved to try what it could do; and as Athena said it was to be a master for mind and mouth, he decided to put it into the mouth of Pegasos.

The next night, Pegasos came again, and Bellerophon walked up to him quietly, this time, and patted him gently, and stroked him, and talked to him as men do to their horses: then suddenly he popped the golden bar into his mouth, and he saw to his surprise that the round part fitted over the head, behind the ears. For as you have guessed already, no doubt, it was a bit and bridle. This was Athena's own invention; for there was none on earth before: men used to pull the horse's mane this way and that, and hope he would go too, or at best they tied a rope round his neck. But they never thought of his mouth.

Pegasos did not seem to mind this new thing in his mouth, but he chewed it contentedly; and suddenly Bellerophon vaulted upon his back, holding the two streamers in his hand. The horse was perfectly quiet. When Bellerophon dug his knees into his flanks, Pegasos spread his wings, and flew up into the sky; and the rider found that he could make him go any way he liked by pulling the rein in that direction. And so, before long, he was soaring over the sea, and before long he was landing in Lycia. He put the horse in a convenient stable, and went to report himself to the King.

Now the King had missed him, for he had not told the King of his dream; and even now he did not tell him about Pegasos, but he only said that he meant to set out soon, and hoped to destroy the monster. The King hardly knew whether he wanted him to succeed, or not.

Then Bellerophon mounted the winged horse, and the horse whinnied with pleasure, and pranced about, and at

a touch of knees and rein, he rose up into the air. Beller-
ophon guided him over the wasted country, until he saw
a dark shape below him, which appeared to be gnawing
some mangled creature upon the ground. Down he
swooped, and it was the monster! Then the monster left his
prey, and looked up: his lion's head croaked and rattled,
his snaky tail hissed and spat poison, and he rose up to re-
ceive his foe.

Bellerophon felt very sick at the smell of the monster,
and the green smoke that came from its mouth, but he
circled round and round until he got a chance—then
swooped down, and pierced its side with his spear. The
monster leapt, Pegasos swerved, and green blood ran from
the monster's side. Again and again Bellerophon pierced it
with his spear, its struggles grew less, and at last it lay still
upon the ground, dead. And as it lay there, the body grad-
ually smouldered away, until there was nothing left but a
heap of grey ashes.

What rejoicings there were when the news went abroad
that the Chimaira was dead! What honours were paid to
Bellerophon when he returned! I need not tell you all his
later adventures. There were others, for Iobatês still tried
to compass his death; but in the end, he was obliged to de-
sist. He gave his daughter to Bellerophon, and now you
might think the man's bad luck was ended. But no! A man's
bad luck is generally in himself, one way or another; and
Bellerophon, after these triumphs, thought himself equal to
the gods.

So he mounted on Pegasos once more, and rode him
straight up to Olympos. When Pegasos once more saw the
divine stables, which he loved, he neighed loudly, and threw
off Bellerophon from his back. Down fell Bellerophon to
the earth! Even a fall like that could not always kill a hero,
and it did not kill Bellerophon; but it maimed him, and
made him a wretched man. For the rest of his life, he wan-
dered about, and kept far from mankind. So pride goeth
before a fall, as Solomon said; and presumptuous pride
was the one thing the Greek gods could not abide.

XXXIX. *Iamos the Pansy-Child*

Heraclês and Theseus were heroes who helped to explore the world, and to clear it of monsters, like those of our own day who have shown how to destroy the little insects which cause yellow fever and malaria.

But I am now to tell you of a hero who left his mark in a different way. There were many like him, for you remember that the souls of the heroes who died in the early ages watched over mankind, and helped good men or punished bad men. My hero to-day is Iamos, the Pansy-child. But why was he called the Pansy-child? You shall hear.

Iamos was doubly a hero; for his mother's father was Poseidon, and his own father was Apollo. His mother, Euadnê, had long dark hair, like the purple of a pansy. She was brought up in the glens of Arcadia, and there she was seen and loved by Apollo, and bore him a son.

She laid the baby down in a thicket; and when the servants found him, he lay in a bed of pansies, purple and golden, and the sunlight shone upon them so that the light itself seemed to be purple and golden. They found two large serpents, with bright eyes, which the gods had sent to feed him; and the serpents fed him with drops of honey from a honey-comb. The voice of Apollo declared, "This child shall be a great prophet, notable above all mankind, and his family shall never fail." His mother gave him the name of Pansy-child, because he was found in the bed of purple-golden pansies.

When he grew up, he went down at dead of night into the river Alpheios, which flowed through Arcadia, by his home, and called aloud upon Poseidon his grandfather, and Apollo his father, and said, "Grant me a people to rule in the world." And his father spoke and said, "Arise, my boy, and follow the sound of my voice." They went along the river, down to a plain through which it flowed to the sea, the place where in future days the city of Olympia was to stand. There Apollo said, "I give you a double treasure of prophecy. At this time, you shall hear the voice which cannot lie; and later, when Heraclês shall come here to found

162

the great games of Olympia, he will establish an oracle of Zeus, and your family, the Pansy clan, shall be always priests of the oracle." And so it befell. The Pansy clan became great and happy, and held their holy place at Olympia, declaring the true mind of Zeus to men.

XL. *The Golden Apple of Discord*

You remember how long ago I told you of Peleus and Thetis, and how Peleus held her fast while she changed into all sorts of shapes. There was a grand wedding feast, you remember, and among the guests were the sea-nymphs, and the gods themselves; but something happened at that feast which I did not tell you. When the invitations were sent, one of the nymphs was left out, and with good reason; for she was Eris, the lady of Discord, as her name denotes, and they did not want discord and quarrels at the wedding feast. But Discord had something to say to that, as you will hear.

Next day two of the sea-nymphs were talking about it: their names were Allspy and Calm, or in Greek, Panopê and Galênê.

Allspy. My dear, did you see what Eris did yesterday, at the feast in Thessaly, because she was not invited?

Calm. No, I was not there; I had to keep the sea calm, you know.

Allspy. Peleus and Thetis had just retired, when Eris crept in unseen, and sent an apple rolling along the floor, a lovely apple, my dear, all of gold! And it had a sentence graven upon it, "For the pretty one!" It rolled where three goddesses were sitting, Hera and Athena and Aphroditê. Hera picked up the apple, and read the words, "For the pretty one!" That's mine! said Hera. No, mine! said Athena. No, no, mine, of course! said Aphroditê. And there was a pretty quarrel! They wanted Zeus to decide, but he said, No, thank you; whichever I give it to, the others will plague my life out. Take it to young Paris of Troy, he is a good judge of beauty.

Calm. And what then?

Allspy. Then the three goddesses went as fast as they could to Troy. I wish I knew what was happening there!

Meanwhile Zeus gave the apple to Hermês, and told him to conduct the goddesses to Mount Ida, where Paris kept his flocks. But first he made the three of them promise to play fair, and to be content with the sentence of the judge. So away they flew. On the way, Aphroditê whispered to Hermês.

Aphroditê. Is he married?

Hermês. Not quite, but he has a sort of wife with him. What made you ask?

Aphroditê. Oh, nothing.

Athena. That's not fair, you are whispering to Hermês.

Hermês. She only asked if Paris were married.

Athena. What's the reason?

Hermês. Oh, nothing, she says.

Athena (to Hermês). I wonder if he is ambitious, and wants to be a great warrior.

Aphroditê. Who's whispering now? I do not complain, you see.

Hermês. There is Mount Ida, and there's the man.

Hera. Where? I can't see anything.

Hermês. There, look along my finger. Do you see those little cows?

Hera. Yes, I see now, I thank you, if that's the man.

Hermês. Yes, that is the man. Let us go down here, and walk up to him, or he will be frightened.—Good day, young man.

Paris. Good day to you, sir. Who are these gentlewomen?

Hermês. They are not women, my dear Paris, but Hera and Athena and Aphroditê. They want you to decide who shall have this apple.

Paris. Let me see it. "For the pretty one." How on earth can a mortal like me decide between goddesses? They are all splendid. When I look at one, I think she is the best, and then if I look at another, I think she is the best.

Hermês. Well, you must do it, for it is the command of Zeus.

Paris. Well, pray them not to be angry with me.

Hermês. They have all promised that.

Paris. Very well, I will do my best; no one can do more.

Pray let me see them one at a time, for they dazzle me all together.

Hermês. Quite right. Go away, you two, and let Hera stay.

Hera. Now, young man, look at my grandeur: and let me tell you, if you vote for me, you shall be King of Asia.

Paris. No bribes for me. Please retire, for I have seen enough now. Athena next, please.

Athena. Here I am. If you vote for me, you shall be a great warrior, always victorious.

Paris. I want no wars and fighting. Peace is what I want. But you shall be none the worse, even if I do not accept your gift. Aphroditê now, please.

Aphroditê. She is here. I see you are young, and handsome, too good to waste in this wilderness. You ought to have a beautiful wife, like Helen.

Paris. Who is Helen?

Aphroditê. A daughter of Zeus himself, and all the noblest young men in the world wooed her, but she chose Meneläos King of Sparta. Vote for me, and you shall have Helen.

Paris. What! When she has a husband already!

Aphroditê. You are simple, indeed. You do not know how these things are managed. All you have to do is to pay them a visit; leave the rest to me.

Paris. I am in love with Helen already! I want to be off.

Aphroditê. Wait, no hurry, let me do my part first.

Paris. And if I give you the apple, you will forget all about me.

Aphroditê. No, I promise you; I will swear an oath if you like.

Paris. Your promise is enough for me. Here is the apple.

So the other two had to make the best of it. And all fell out as Aphroditê had said. Paris paid a visit to Sparta; Helen fell in love with him at once, for she had been maddened by Aphroditê; and Helen left her husband, and followed Paris to Troy.

Then King Meneläos of Sparta, and King Agamemnon his brother, made a league of all the cities in Greece; and a great fleet sailed to Troy, and a great army laid siege to it. For ten years the siege lasted, and then Troy was taken, and burnt, and razed to the ground. There lay the ruins for three thousand years, until quite a short time ago, an explorer dug them up, and now you can see for yourself the marks of the fire upon the old stones. And how many thousands of men lost their lives, and how much misery was caused by the golden apple of Discord! Some of the stories of this great siege you shall hear before long.

XLI. *The Arms of Achillês*

But now we are coming into the history of men, rather than gods. By this time, the gods are well established, and manage the world regularly enough; but the stories are more about men, and the gods come in occasionally.

The apple of Discord, as I told you, was the cause of a dreadful war; and one of the great men in this war was Achillês, whom you remember as a baby in the arms of Cheiron's wife. Achillês was a magnificent warrior, and a generous man, but he had his faults, like the rest of us. One of them was a fierce pride, which would not put up with the smallest slight, if he thought it touched his honour. And King Agamemnon had insulted him. We cannot go into the whole story now; but the upshot was, that Achillês retired to his tent, and said, "Very well, you may fight your battles yourself. I did not come here to be insulted, and I hope you will be well beaten."

You see, they had both lost their temper. I do not make any excuse for either of them; I am just telling the story.

When Achillês the champion would not fight, the Trojans took heart, and really did beat off the Greeks; indeed, they got as far as the Greek ships by the shore, and set a number of them on fire. Achillês was deeply distressed at this, for he did not really want the Trojans to win. But he would not make friends again, and say that he had gone too far. "I said I would not fight," he told them, "and I will not fight. But I will lend my armour to my friend Patroclos, and when the Trojans see it, they will think he is Achillês, and run away."

So Patroclos put on the armour of Achillês. Then there was a great fight; but in the end Patroclos was himself killed by Hector of Troy, and Hector carried off the armour of Achillês.

This was too much for Achillês. He loved Patroclos more than he hated Agamemnon, so he determined to avenge him. But where was his armour? In the enemy's hands. He poured dust on his head, and cried aloud: and his mother heard it in the depths of the sea, Thetis his mother, the sea-nymph. She cried to her friends around her, the other nymphs of the sea, "I hear my son's voice, and I know he will die! Did I not tell him that he would die, if he came to this cruel war? Be happy at home, I said, and live long; for if you go to the war, your life shall be glorious, but your days shall be few. And he chose glory and few days! I will go and see what troubles him."

She left her cave, and came to the shore, and called aloud, "My son, why do you weep? Tell me, and hide it not. If the Greeks are defeated, that is what you prayed for."

He answered, "I did so, but what do I care for that? My dear friend is dead, whom I loved as my own life. Hector killed him! Hector has my beautiful armour! I do not wish to live, if I may not kill Hector with my own hands!"

She said, "Ah, my boy, when Hector dies, your death must soon follow."

He said, "I care not. I wish I could die now."

She said, "Well, if you must fight, I will go and bring back new armour for you, from Hephaistos himself."

Then Thetis made her way to Olympos, and came to the house of Hephaistos. He was busy in the forge, but his wife said, "What brings you here, Thetis, my dear friend? You do not often pay us a visit."

She led her to a seat, and called out, "Husband, come this way. Thetis has something to ask you."

Hephaistos said, "Indeed she is one whom I respect, and I am grateful to her, because she took care of me when I was thrown out of heaven. What pretty things I used to make for her in those days! Brooches, and necklaces, and all sorts of gewgaws, in the cave under the sea, and nobody knew where I was!"

He put down his tools, and wiped his face and chest with a sponge, and put on a clean vest, and hobbled in; and two waiting women attended upon him, made by himself;

they were made all of gold, but they could speak, and they could understand what he said to them. He clasped Thetis by the hand, and said, "What brings you here, Thetis my dear friend? You do not often pay us a visit. Say what you want, and it shall be done, if I can do it."

She said, "Hephaistos, is there any one of the Olympians whom Zeus has treated so badly as me? He gave me a mortal husband, who is now old and useless in his palace; I did not want him. I had a lovely son, and I had to let him go to the war at Troy. I shall never see him at home again, never find him a wife! And now his friend has been killed, and his armour is lost. That is what brings me here. I beg you to make him shield, and helmet, and breastplate, and greaves, for those which were lost along with his friend."

"Set your mind at rest," said the smith. "You shall have them, and a fine sight they shall be!"

And a fine sight they were when Thetis presented them to her son. He was amazed, and all his men were amazed. And he put on the armour, and went out to the fight. He met, and he conquered, his great enemy Hector, and the Greeks once more prevailed.

But as his mother foretold, his death followed soon after. He was killed by an arrow shot by Paris, which hit him in the heel. That is the place where his mother held him, if you remember, when she bathed him in the Styx to make him invulnerable. We often use the words, "the heel of Achillês," to mean a weak spot in anyone, which comes from this story.

XLII. *Arês in Battle*

In the siege of Troy, the gods took sides, and often quarrelled about it. Aphroditê of course was on the side of Paris, and so was her lover, Arês; Hera and Athena, of course, were against Paris. Zeus kept them in order as well as he could, and tried to be fair, but they would keep on meddling. And sometimes the gods became so excited, that they joined in themselves. One of these times I am going to tell you about.

Athena had a great favourite among the Greeks, named

Diomêdês, and she encouraged him to go into battle.
"Fight, and fear not," she said, "I will be near you. But
keep clear of the gods, if you see any on the field. Only
Aphroditê you may wound a little, if you happen to meet
her: leave the others alone."

So Diomêdês went into the fray. Before long, he had a
fight with Aineias, the man who was to escape from Troy,
and afterwards to found the Roman people. Diomêdês
wounded Aineias and would have killed him, but his
mother saved him; Aphrodité herself was his mother, and
she laid her arms round him, and he was carried to his
chariot.

Then Diomêdês went straight for Aphroditê, since he
knew that she was no fighter, and wounded her on the
hand. The gods have not blood, like men, but they have
something instead in their veins, and that something ran
out, and she gave a shriek. Diomêdês shouted out:

"Away from the battle, daughter of Zeus! Is it not
enough that you are a plague to women? Leave war alone,
or you shall shiver when you hear the word!"

Aphroditê ran out of the battle, to the place where
Arês was sitting and looking on. She cried out, "Dear
brother, save me, and lend me your horses to go home!
I have a dreadful wound, which a mortal man has dealt
me!"

Arês helped her into his car, and Iris took the reins,
and drove her up to Olympos. And Aphroditê ran to her
mother, and fell upon her lap. Her mother threw her arms
round her, and said, "Who has done this to you, dear
child?" She answered, "I was wounded by a man, Dio-
mêdês, when I was saving my son. These Greeks are not
content with fighting Trojans, you see they fight with us
too!"

"Bear up, my child!" her mother said. "We all have our
troubles from these troublesome men. Think how Arês
was shut up in a brazen jar for thirteen months. Think how
Hera was hit by Heraclês with an arrow. Think how the
same Heraclês shot Hadês himself with another. As for
Diomêdês, he shall soon be sorry he attacked one of the
immortals!" And she wiped the wound clean, and cured
the pain.

But Athena and Hera made fun of her, and said, "Look,

father Zeus, see Aphroditê has been with her friends, the Trojan women, and scratched her finger on some one's brooch!"

Meanwhile the battle went on furiously; for Arês himself was ranging about, and urging on the Trojans to fight. Hera complained to Zeus that this was not fair; so Zeus said:

"Very well, go down and tell him to stop."

Then Hera and Athena drove down to the field. Athena found Diomêdês wounded, and said, "What, not fighting? I see you are not the man your father was."

"I did fight," he said, "and I wounded Aphroditê; but I came away when I found that Arês was taking a hand, because you told me to leave the gods alone, except Aphroditê. And now I am wounded too."

"Fear nothing," said Athena, "not even Arês himself. Go in again, and I will be with you. Go, and strike that false traitor himself! He promised us to fight against the Trojans, and now he is helping them." So saying, she drove him in his car to the battle-field. She put on her head the cap of Hadês, that she might become invisible.

When Arês saw Diomêdês, he threw his spear at him, but Athena caught it, and guided it harmless away. Then Diomêdês lunged with his spear at Arês; and Athena guided it straight, so that it pierced his flank, and came out at the back. Diomêdês pulled out the spear, and Arês roared as loud as nine or ten thousand men roaring together.

Almost before they could look, Arês was gone: like a black whirlwind of dust he shot through the air, and in a moment he was beside the throne of Zeus, and pointing to the immortal blood that flowed from his wound. He said in a complaining tone:

"Father Zeus, do not you mind seeing crimes like this? We gods are always suffering horrors, all for the sake of men. It is the fault of that crazy girl of yours, Athena, curse her. The rest of us obey you, but she does just what she likes, and you take no notice. Now she has made that overbearing young Diomêdês attack the immortal gods. He wounded Aphroditê first, and now look at me! If I had not a quick pair of feet, I should be lying amid a heap of corpses."

Zeus frowned at him, and said, "Do not come whimpering here to me, you facing-both-ways! I hate you worse than any god in Olympos. All you care for is battle and sudden death. You have your mother's hard temper, unendurable. I will not put up with it. If you were not my own son, you should have been long ago the lowest of the immortals."

Then he left Arês to get his wound cured, and to be petted by his mother, Hera.

I cannot help thinking that the poet who told this tale was poking fun at the gods a little. But they were a kindly race, and could all take a joke against themselves, except perhaps Artemis. One of them at least, Dionysos, had a theatre in later days, where comic plays were acted; and these often made fun of the god himself, with the high priest sitting in the chief chair of honour, and laughing with the rest. But the god took it all in good part.

What they could not abide, was pride, and presumptuousness. For men were always becoming puffed up, and pretending to be equal with the gods; and there was some excuse, when so many of them were sons of the gods. One man, the brother of Sisyphos, claimed to have sacrifices paid to himself, and imitated the thunder and lightning of Zeus; but Zeus visited him with the real lightning. Even the gentle Leto, gentlest of all the immortals, was roused to anger by Niobê. Niobê was the daughter of Tantalos, whom you saw in the dark house of Hadês, standing in a lake. She had six fine sons and six lovely daughters, and she boasted that she was superior to Leto, who had only twins. Nor was she inferior in birth, for Tantalos was the son of Zeus. This infuriated the gentle Leto, who complained to her twins, Apollo and Artemis. They shot all the sons and daughters of Niobê with their arrows. Niobê wept for her children, until she herself was turned into stone. You may see her figure still, in the mountains near Smyrna, with the tears ever running down her cheeks, as the dew and the rain distil upon her head.

XLIII. *Odysseus*

At last the Trojan war was over; it is a long story, well worth your hearing, but I cannot tell it all now. I must tell you, however, of the adventures of one of the men who went home.

This was Odysseus of Ithaca. Now Ithaca is a small and rocky island, which lies in the sea west of Greece, not far south of Corfu. All the islands in this group once belonged to England, only we gave them back to the King of Greece after the Greeks made themselves free of the Turks. It is a lovely island, full of flowers, and the people are kind, and still very proud of their great man, Odysseus, after three thousand years.

Odysseus had left behind him his wife, named Penelopê, whom he loved so much that all he wanted was to go home again and be at peace. When he bade good-bye to her, and his baby son Telemachos, he said, "My wife, I may be killed in the war. If I die, bring up our son to be a good man, and when he is old enough to manage the house, I hope you will marry again and be happy." But she said, "My husband, I want no one but you." He was away for twenty years: the siege lasted for ten years, and he took ten years to get home, but when he arrived, he found her waiting for him. And this is the story.

Odysseus set sail from Troy with his countrymen of Ithaca and the islands round about, twelve ships in all. They were blown far away to the west of the Mediterranean Sea, and when the wind fell, they came to land in a lovely country. The people welcomed those who went on shore, and gave them to eat of the fruit of the country, the lotus, which they lived on, sweet as honey. Anyone who ate of it wished never to come away, but only to go on for ever eating the sweet lotus. It seemed to be always afternoon, and nobody wanted to do any more work for ever and ever. But Odysseus would not have that. He carried off the lazy men, and tied them down under the benches, until the ships were well away.

By and by the wind took them to a little wild island,

and Odysseus went off with one ship to explore. As he came near the mainland, he saw an enclosure upon the hillside, full of sheep and goats; so he took a few men with him, and climbed up to the place. They found a great cave within the walls of the enclosure. There were pens for lambs, and pens for kids: rows and rows of cheeses, pans and jars full of whey or milk. They helped themselves to milk and cheese, and roasted a lamb, and enjoyed themselves.

By and by a horrible monster approached, big and hairy, and they ran and hid in the cave. He milked all the sheep and goats, and curdled the milk: then he lit a fire, and saw the men.

"Who are you, stranger?" he asked.

Odysseus said, "Sir, we are strangers from Troy; have pity on us, for Zeus is the god of strangers."

"Pooh, pooh!" he said—"Zeus! We care nothing for Zeus, or any gods: we are stronger than they are."

He stretched out his hands, and caught two of the men, and dashed them like puppies on the ground, so that their brains ran out. Then he carved them limb from limb, and ate them for his supper, and slept.

This monster was a Cyclops, named Polyphemos. You remember that dreadful brood of creatures, and the three who were guardians of fire in the early days.

Next morning, the Cyclops killed and ate two more men, and went about his work. But he rolled a huge stone in front of the cave, so that no one could get out.

But Odysseus was never at a loss for a plan. He picked up a sapling of olive wood which lay in the cave, and smoothed it, and made it ready; and he chose out four good men to help him, when the night should come.

In the evening, the Cyclops drove in all his rams, and rolled the great stone in front of the door; next, as before, he killed and ate two more men for supper. Then Odysseus came up to him, bearing a skin of wine which he had brought from the ship, and he said, "Cyclops, here, have a drink after your supper!"

He drank it, and it pleased him so much that he said, "Another, please!" Odysseus gave him another, and another still, and he said, "Indeed, this is fine stuff, better than our wine! I must give you a stranger's gift for this. What is your name?"

"My name," said Odysseus, "is Noman."

"Very well, Noman, your gift shall be, that I will eat you last of all."

Then he lay down, and went to sleep, grunting and growling.

There was Odysseus, and there were his men, shut up in the cave, and they could not get out; for the stone was too heavy for them to move. But Odysseus had his plan ready.

He took the olive-sapling, and buried it under the ashes; and when it was red hot, he made his four men hold it straight, while he pushed the point hard into the eye of the Cyclops; for he has only one eye, as you remember, in the middle of his forehead, with a thick bushy eyebrow running right across his face. The red-hot point burnt the eyeball, which sizzled like fat in the fire.

The Cyclops roared aloud, and pulled out the stake, and threw it from him, and the men ran off and hid in the corners of the cave. The Cyclops made such a noise, that all the other Cyclôpês came running up to the cave, and called out, "Why are you making all that noise? Is anyone killing you?" Polyphemos replied, "Noman is killing me!" Then they said, "If no man is killing you, you must just pray to God; what is the use of waking us all out of our sleep?" And they went away, but Odysseus laughed to himself at the success of his trick.

Then he caught up the long withies that lay on the floor in a heap, and tied his men each under one of the fleecy rams, with another ram tied to this ram on each side. He picked the biggest ram of all for himself, and waited for morning.

In the morning, the Cyclops rolled back the stone from the door of the cave, and let his rams out, holding out his hands, and feeling their backs; but he did not feel underneath, so the men all got safely out, fastened together in threes. Odysseus came last, hanging on underneath the biggest ram of all. And so they escaped from the Cyclops. But this Cyclops was a son of Poseidon, and ever afterwards Poseidon hated Odysseus and did his best to destroy him.

They all sailed away, until they reached the island of Aiolos, the steward of the winds. Aiolos wished to help Odysseus on his way; so he bottled up all the winds in a leather bag, except the West Wind, which was to blow them home. They went bowling along for nine days, until they actually came in sight of Ithaca, their home; and then Odysseus, tired out, fell asleep.

While he was asleep, the sailors eyed this bag, and one said to another, "I wonder what Aiolos gave him. Gold and silver, to be sure! Let us see." So they opened the mouth of the bag, and all the winds poured out, and began to blow together, north, south, east, and west, and blew them far away. They had many adventures, which I cannot tell of now, but after a long time they came to land in a pleasant island, and Odysseus sent some of his men to explore.

They found a fine house among the trees; and as they came near, what should they see but all sorts of animals, lions and tigers, leopards and wild boars, which did them no harm; they just ran up, wagging their tails, and barking in a friendly way. The men all went in, except one, who remained to watch.

Within the hall was a woman, singing sweetly as she plied the loom. She gave them welcome, and provided a good feast; and when they had eaten, she tapped each with her stick, and said, "Away to the sty with you!" At once their hair changed into bristles, and they turned into pigs, and ran away into the sty.

The watcher reported to Odysseus that the others had all disappeared; and Odysseus himself went to explore. On the way, he met the god Hermês, who gave him a magic root which would protect him against enchantments. So when he came to the house of Circê—that was the witch's name—she had no power over him, and he compelled her to change his men back to their proper shape.

Circê was a good friend to them after this, and helped them with advice, and gave them all they wanted. Odysseus had to visit the dark Kingdom of Hadês, where he received directions for his homeward voyage. And on the way back he had many other dangers to face.

He had to pass by the island of the Sirens. These were witches who looked like birds; they sang so sweetly, that every one who heard them felt obliged to land. There they sat in a meadow, singing, and all round them were the shrivelled bodies of the men who had come to hear, and sat down and listened, until they died. Odysseus was warned of this by Circê; and before he came to the island, he plugged up all the ears of all his men with wax, so that they should not hear. But he wanted to hear himself, yet not to be hurt; so he told his men to tie him to the mast, and not to let him loose, whatever happened.

Then they rowed on. Soon the lovely song of the Sirens was heard, and Odysseus struggled to get free, and shouted to his men to let him loose; but they rowed on, until they were safe out of hearing.

Next they had to pass between Scylla and Charybdis. On one side of a strait was Charybdis, where a whirlpool three times a day sucked up the water, and spouted it out again: no ship could live in that whirlpool. On the other side was a rock, and on this rock in a cave lived a monster, Scylla, with twelve legs, and six long necks with heads like dogs; and if a ship passed by, she curled down her six necks, and caught up a sailor with each head. This is what she did to Odysseus and his crew.

After this, all his ships were destroyed in a frightful storm, but Odysseus himself was saved, and washed up on another island. On this island lived another witch, Calypso, who saved him, and kept him there for seven long years. She wanted him for a husband, and she offered to make him immortal; but he refused, because all he wanted was to return to his beloved wife Penelopê. And he did return, and did find his wife waiting for him, although he had to fight a terrible battle with his enemies before he won her again. But after all his troubles, he spent with his wife a peaceful and quiet old age.

XLIV. *Cupid and Psychê*

You remember Cupid, the mischievous and disobedient boy, who shot his arrows at Medeia, and how he was ready to shoot anyone for a toy, or just for fun. Cupid

by and by began to grow up, and then fell in love himself!
Here is the story.

The King and Queen of a certain place, whose name I
do not know, had three daughters. The two elder daughters
were nothing in particular; but the youngest was the most
beautiful creature ever born. She was so beautiful, that
people thought she must be Aphroditê herself come to
earth. They came to look at her in crowds, and showered
flowers upon her as she passed by. The worshippers no
longer frequented the temples of Aphroditê, but turned
to this new goddess. Her name was Psychê, which means
the Soul.

Aphroditê saw that her temples were deserted, and no
sacrifices were paid to her; and she became jealous and
angry. She called her boy Cupid, and said to him, "Do you
see how your mother is neglected? Insulted? Pushed aside
for a mortal? Go and shoot one of your arrows at her,
so that she may fall in love with the ugliest and meanest
man in the world!"

Cupid was still not too old for mischief, so he only
said, "All right, mother!" and off he flew.

Meanwhile the King, Psychê's father, was in trouble,
and did not know what to do. His two elder daughters
were soon married, but no one wanted to marry Psychê.
She was too high for them, they only scattered flowers and
offered prayers. So he enquired of the oracle of Apollo;
and Aphroditê had already persuaded Apollo to help
her. The god replied, "It is her fate to be married to a
dragon. You must lay her out on a bier, as if she were
dead, and place her on the hill which overlooks a deep
valley near your town."

While this was preparing, Cupid flew by, and saw her.
He needed no arrow, and he shot none, but he fell head-
over-ears in love at first sight. Then he laid his plans.

When the funeral procession was ready, Psychê was
carried out, and laid on the hill-top; and the people re-
turned home lamenting sadly. But when they were gone,
the South Wind blew strong and gentle, and lifted up
Psychê from the bier, and carried her to the bottom of the
valley, where he left her sleeping peacefully on a bed of
flowers.

Psychê woke up, and could not make out where she

was. Then she rose, and wandered about, until she found a beautiful house, full of gold and marble, but not a soul to be seen. She saw a table, covered with all sorts of food, and sat down by it. Then a voice was heard from the air, "Fear nothing, my lady, all you see is yours, and we are your servants to wait upon you." Whatever she wanted, the unseen servants read her thought, and the viands seemed to come of themselves to her hands. In the evening, there was beautiful music and singing, but still no one to be seen. Then she went to bed, and slept.

In the middle of the night, she awoke, and felt some one by her side. "I suppose this is the dragon!" she thought, and shuddered. But when she plucked up courage to put out her hand, she felt a soft face, and soft flowing hair, and a voice said, "I am your husband, Psychê, do not be afraid. I am yours, and this place is yours; only one thing I must ask you—never try to see me, or great trouble will follow." They talked pleasantly for a long time, and Psychê told him all her strange adventures. Then she fell asleep; and in the morning, there was no one there.

But naturally enough she was dull with no one to talk to, and no one to see her lovely house. So one night she begged her husband to let her sisters pay her a visit. He did not want to agree; but at last he said, "Very well, if you must have them, I will bring them to you; but be careful to tell them nothing about me."

Then he sent the South Wind, and the wind caught up her sisters, and wafted them softly down to her door. Imagine their astonishment to see this grand house, and Psychê ready to welcome them! They went round, and looked at everything, and asked all sorts of questions. In particular, they wanted to know where her husband was.

She said first, "He is hunting," and then in her excitement she forgot all about that, and said, "Oh, he has some weighty business to do." The sisters were jealous and suspicious, and at last one said, "I don't believe you have a husband at all! I believe he is that old dragon, and you are ashamed to show him!"

This made Psychê angry, but she blurted out the truth, how he came only at night, and she never saw him, but he was certainly no dragon.

"How do you know," said the elder sister, "if you have never seen him? I'll tell you what. Put a lamp in your cupboard, and a sharp knife. When he is asleep, just take a look, and if he is the dragon, cut off his head, and you will be safe."

Psychê was a simple soul, and agreed; and the South Wind wafted the sisters home again.

So that night Psychê hid a lamp in the cupboard, with a sharp knife; and in the middle of the night, when her husband was asleep, she got up softly, and opened the cupboard, and took the knife in her right hand, and the lamp in her left, and turned to look at her husband. What did she see but a beautiful boy, with flowing hair, and most wonderful of all, a pair of wings, green and gold, folded over his shoulders! For of course you have guessed long ago that he was no other than Cupid. She was so much amazed, that she let a drop of hot oil drop from the lamp upon Cupid's arm, and it burnt him, and he awoke. Then he saw his beloved Psychê, with a sharp knife in her hand!

"You wicked thing!" he cried. "Do you want to murder me in my sleep?"

"Oh, no, no," she said, as the tears ran from her eyes. "I only wanted to see that you had not turned into a dragon."

"Do I look like a dragon?" said Cupid. "Did I feel like a dragon, when I put my arms round you and kissed you? Well, I told you that you must not see me, and you promised and now you have broken your promise I must fly away, and I do not suppose you will see me again."

With these words, he spread his wings, and flew out of the open window.

Now Psychê was in despair. She had done wrong, and she knew it, and all her happy life was at an end. However, as life was nothing to her without her husband, she set out to tramp all over the world, and find him, or at least to die, and have no more trouble.

So she tramped over hill and dale; she tore her clothes in the brambles, and wounded her feet on the stones, but no trace could she find of Cupid.

Now Aphroditê knew quite well what was going on, and she thought she would like to enjoy the sight of

Psychê, humbled and sorry. So she sent out Hermês, the crier of the gods, who cried all over the country, "Oyez oyez oyez! Lost, stolen, or strayed, one slave-girl of our lady Aphroditê, answers to the name of Psychê. Reward for finding, one kiss to the finder!" Everybody was agog to win such a prize; and in the end, some one found Psychê, wandering about, and brought her to Aphroditê's door.

When she was taken before Aphroditê, the goddess said, "So here is the proud girl who set up to be my rival. She does not look much now, but as she is my slave, let us see if she can do any work. You there, get the job ready," and she signalled to some of her servants.

They went into the next room, and there they brought baskets of seed and grains, wheat, oats, and barley, millet and mustard, thistledown and all the seeds of all the weeds in the garden. They poured them all on to the ground, and mixed them up, and there was a great heap of everything so that you could not tell what was what. Then Psychê was brought in, and Aphroditê said, "Sort them out, and let them be ready by sunset."

There was a task! Was ever anyone set to do a task like that? Psychê knew she could not do it; so she sat down in the corner, and covered up her head with her robe, and waited for whatever might happen.

But there was an ant in the corner, who heard and saw all that was done. He was delighted at the sight of these heaps of corn and seed, but he was a kind ant, and he felt very sorry for poor Psychê. "Look here, wife," said he, "let us sort them out for the young lady. Hullo, you fellows!" he shouted to the other ants. "Here's a treasure for us! We have to sort them all out, and then we may take whatever we like." Out came the ants in swarms, from every hole, till the heap of seeds was black with them. They made quick work of it. Long before sunset the seeds were all sorted into heaps, and the army of ants went away, with as much as they could carry for their own store.

And when Psychê looked up, there were all the seeds in little heaps, wheat, and barley, and oats, and mustard, and thistledown, each in its own heap.

Aphroditê was not at all pleased to find her task done;

but she had nothing to say, so she gave Psychê a crust of bread, and told her there would be other work on the morrow.

Indeed, she set Psychê many strange tasks, which somehow or other she always managed to do; and at the last she said, "Well, you are a better work-woman than I thought. I have only one thing more, and if you can do that, I will set you free. Take this casket; and go down to the dark world of Hadês, and give it to Queen Persephonê, and ask her to send me an ounce of her beauty; for I have lost a lot of mine, through nursing my poor son Cupid, who is ill with a bad burn on his arm."

Psychê took the casket. She went into the dark cavern, and through the dark tunnel where Orpheus had passed, and into the dark house of Hadês. She gave the casket to Persephonê, and received a jar from her; and set out on her last journey homeward. Through the dark tunnel she came, and out of the dark cavern; and as she came into the light of day, she felt weary, and lay down to rest.

"What is in this jar?" she thought. "An ounce of beauty? Perhaps she might spare some for me; then I might be more beautiful in my husband's eyes, if I were to see him again." She opened the jar. And what was in the jar? I suppose Aphroditê had put some message in the casket; for there was no ounce of beauty in the jar. Out of it came a stream of smoky mist, and it got into Psychê's lungs, and choked her, and she fell back unconscious.

But what was Cupid doing all this time? He was ill in bed with the burn on his arm, which had come from Psychê's hot oil; and Aphroditê his mother, who was nursing him, kept him locked up in his room, that he might not get into any more mischief. But she forgot the window. Now Cupid's wound was well, and he got up, and he thought he would try his wings, to see if they were stiff after lying there so long. So he flew out of the window.

Cupid found his wingers were all right. He flew about until he spied a bundle lying at the mouth of the dark cave. He was a little curious to know what this bundle was, and flew closer. What was his surprise to see his own Psychê, unconscious and pale as death!

One puff of immortal breath from his lips, and the misty fog dispersed, and Psychê opened her eyes and saw Cupid.

Then indeed there was rejoicing. Psychê told Cupid all her adventures, and this last one, and then remembering, she said, "And I opened the bottle! But I must finish my errand, and deliver it to the lady Aphroditê."

"Very well," says Cupid, "I will go with you." And they went together to his mother, and Psychê gave her the jar, but said nothing about opening it.

Aphroditê was not at all pleased, but she could not hold out any longer when Cupid said, "Mother, this is my wife." She answered, "That is all very well, but if you care nothing for your mother, you cannot marry without the consent of Father Zeus." "Then we'll get it!" said Cupid, and caught up Psychê in his arms, and spread his wings, and flew up to the throne of Zeus.

He told Zeus the whole story: how he had been sent to shoot an arrow at Psychê, and had fallen in love himself; about the plan he made to win her, before the dragon could find her; what terrible hardships Psychê had gone through; what tasks she had done; and how Cupid had found her again. Zeus was rather pleased at the story, and said, "You are a young rogue, but if you really want to marry and settle down into a respectable member of Olympos, I will not make any objection." So there was a fine wedding feast; all the gods were happy, and even Aphroditê was made a friend, when for a wedding present, Zeus gave Psychê the gift of immortality.

XLV. *Great Pan Is Dead*

I daresay you will wonder why I tell you nothing of our own ancestors, or the French, or Germans, or Russians. The reason is, that they were of no account; they were just savages, and their gods were monsters, who have perished off the earth and left hardly a trace behind; only their names remain in the names Tuesday, Wednesday, Thursday and Friday. They were not worthy of the notice of the Greek gods, so the gods took no wives from them. These nations were preparing for their parts in the history of the world, but the time was not yet come. The Indians, it is true, had a large family of gods who were distantly related to the Greeks, but it is too long a story to tell of them now. I must pass on to the end of the Greek gods, for their end was approaching.

In a far-off corner of the world there was a small nation, unnoticed or despised, who had a special God of their own; a terrible God, and quite different from the Greeks, for he could tolerate no other god. Clouds and darkness were round about him, righteousness and judgment were the habitation of his seat; a fire went out before him, and burnt up his enemies round about. And after many hundreds of years, there came one from him who was called Jesus Christ, a God of goodwill and a Prince of peace. This religion, which seemed to the Greeks foolish and contemptible, spread all over the world where the Greek gods ruled, and it took their power from them. The temples of the old gods were taken to be churches for the new God, and named after his holy saints. For the priests of the new God were wise men. They only changed what was bad in the old religion, and took over many of its feasts, such as Christmas and Easter, which they joined with the Christian feasts. They chose the patron saints of the churches so as to remind the Greeks of their old gods, in order that they might feel at home with them. Thus at Athens, the great temple of Athena, the maiden goddess, became the church of the Virgin Mary; the temple of Theseus became the church of St. George. St. Elias, that is Elijah the prophet, took over the temples of Helios, the sun-god, because the names were alike: the temples of Helios were on the tops of the hills, and there you may see now the chapels of St. Elias. St. Demetrios took the place of Demeter. And there was a group of three very ancient gods, which had shrines in Delos and Athens and elsewhere; they were called the Three Fathers, and their shrines now became sacred to the Holy Trinity. The sick people who used to worship Asclepios now turned to those saints who cared for healing; and they made the same offerings of gratitude in the churches as they used to do. You may still see in the churches silver models of arms, legs, and teeth, made by people who have had them cured.

One evening, when this great change was taking place, a traveller set sail from Greece to Italy. The wind fell, and the ship was becalmed, while it was making its way through the crowd of little islands off the west coast; and it drifted close to the island of Paxos. The passengers had all dined, and they were lounging about on deck, when from the island a loud voice was heard crying out— "Thamûs!" This did amaze them, for Thamûs was the name of the steersman. He did not answer, and a second cry came—"Thamûs!" and a third—"Thamûs!"

Then the steersman did answer, "Ahoy! What is it?" and the voice rejoined, "When you come over against Palôdês, tell them that Great Pan is dead!"

This caused much excitement, and they all debated whether to go there or not. At last the steersman said, "If there is a wind, I will sail straight on; but if we drift near the place, I will give the news."

The wind came not, they drifted on; and by and by the ship was over against the place. The steersman went into the bows of the ship, and called in a loud voice towards the land, "Great Pan is dead!"

Immediately they heard a loud noise on shore, weeping and wailing and lamentation; and a wind sprang up, and they sailed away on their voyage.

Great Pan really was dead, and so were all the Olympian gods. They were not immortal, as they thought. They played their part in the world's history, and passed away. Of all that mighty company, two only are left. One we will no longer call Cupid, for he has grown up, and he has turned out to be no other than that strange and wonderful Eros, or Love, who appeared at the very first out of Chaos, no one knew how, and still remains as the spirit of the new religion. The other is Psychê, or the soul of man, who has been taken up into heaven and made immortal.

PRONOUNCING INDEX

The names throughout the book are spelt as the Greeks spelt them, except a few which are common in English, such as Cupid, or Delphi and Aegina.

Two dots as on ö, or the mark on ê, mean that it is a separate syllable.

The list shows how you may pronounce the names. Sound the letters as in English, but c is always sounded as k; ch as kh; g is always as in gas, not like j; eu sounds like you, for instance in Per-seus, O-dys´-seus, etc.

The mark over ā, ē, ī, ō, ū, means that, if you wish to be quite correct, it should be sounded as a long vowel.

Be careful, when you say the names, to keep the accent in the right place. It is marked ´.

185

GENEALOGICAL CHART

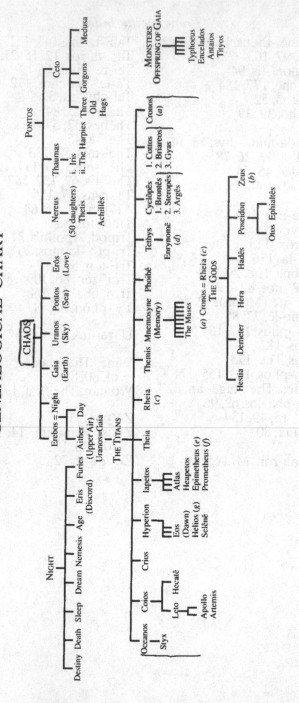

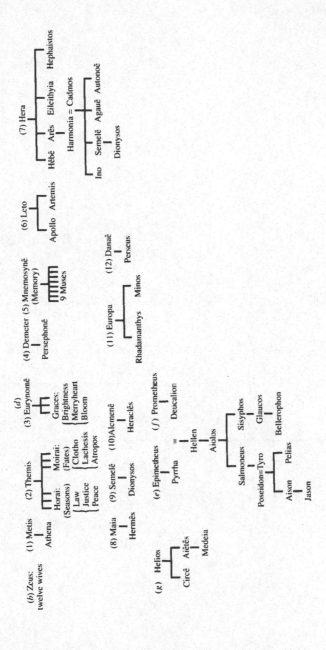

(b) Zeus: twelve wives

(1) Metis
— Athena

(2) Themis
— Horai: (Seasons) — Law / Justice / Peace
— Moirai: (Fates) — Clotho / Lachesis / Atropos

(d) (3) Eurynomê
— Graces: Brightness / Merryheart / Bloom

(4) Demeter
— Persephonê

(5) Mnemosynê (Memory)
— 9 Muses

(6) Leto
— Apollo / Artemis

(7) Hera
— Hêbê / Arês / Eileithyia / Hephaistos
Harmonia = Cadmos
— Ino / Semelê / Agauê / Autonoê
Dionysos

(8) Maia
— Hermês

(9) Semelê
— Dionysos

(10) Alcmenê
— Heraclês

(11) Europa
— Rhadamanthys / Minos

(12) Danaê
— Perseus

(e) Epimetheus
Pyrrha =
(f) Prometheus
— Deucalion
Hellen
— Salmoneus / Aiolos
Poseidon = Tyro
— Aison / Pelias
Jason
Sisyphos / Glaucos
Bellerophon

(g) Helios
— Circê / Aiêtês
Medeia